Beautiful

on the

Mountains

By the same author:

Spiritual Detox

Life: What's That About?

What Is Your Problem?

Searching for God

Rhythm of Life

There Is No Shortage!

Grief Encounter

Stranger in the Mirror

A Word About Your Healing

That's the Spirit!

Beautiful

on the

Mountains

DON EGAN

ISBN   978-0-9554390-3-2

Scripture quotations, unless otherwise indicated, are
from the New King James Version.

Used with permission.

Published by

The RSVP Trust

P O Box 55, Stowmarket, Suffolk, IP14 1UG, England

www.rsvptrust.co.uk

In memory of
Peter & Barbara Egan.

This is the true story of my life.
However, the names of some people and places
have been changed or omitted to protect the
identities of individuals.

*"How beautiful upon the mountains
are the feet of him who brings good news."*
(Isaiah 52:7)

*"Who am I, O Sovereign Lord, and what is my
family, that you have brought me this far?"*
(2 Samuel 7:18)

Contents

Chapter 1

Appointment in Rwanda

As the army pick-up truck bumped up the steep Rwandan mountain track, Norman Desire, our interpreter, was having an animated conversation with the soldier who was driving. It was all in Kinyarwanda, the national language of Rwanda, so I understood nothing of what was being said. I looked out of the window across the lush, green mountains of Kibungo district and wondered what the day would bring.

We were on our way to find a genocide site, at my request. It was three years after the 1994 genocide and Rwanda was still unstable. I had addressed crowds in Africa many times but that had been in neighbouring Uganda, where there had been thirteen years of relative peace, at least in Kampala.

My friend, Charles Mugisha, who sat next to me in the truck, had urged me to come to Rwanda and speak about finding hope in the face of grief, loss and death. Despite my own loss years earlier, I felt less than qualified. So before I preached anywhere in Rwanda, I wanted to go and stand where the people of this nation once stood. I wanted to stand in the midst of their loss and grief. I wanted, in some small way, to touch the deep wound of the genocide that had crippled this beautiful country. I wanted to obey the instruction of Jesus, to weep with those who weep.

As the road levelled off, we passed the ruins of many homes destroyed by war. Ladies, carrying baskets of bananas on their heads, stared at my white face as we drove past. The soldier, sitting on the back of the truck, became more alert and took hold of his automatic rifle. There were still some snipers in these mountains and we had been given this armed escort for our protection. My good friend, Adam Waller, was accompanying me on this trip and I wondered what effect all this was having on him.

Presently, we came to the Catholic Church at Nyarubuye. The straining engine of the truck finally rested from its torturous climb up the mountain and fell silent as we stopped outside the church. Some ladies were singing in the church and their song drifted out of the red brick building through the warm air. A white statue of Jesus stood with open arms above the main door. We climbed out of the vehicle and someone went to find the priest.

Three years earlier, journalist Fergal Keane had stood on this very spot, during a Panorama programme, and shown the world the horrors of the Rwandan genocide. An estimated one million men, women and children had died at the hands of their neighbours in one hundred days of hell on earth.

These areas were still very sensitive and we needed permission from the government to be here, which we had arranged the day before in a meeting with the Minister for Culture. Our friend, Norman

Desire, was well connected with some members of the government, which had helped in arranging this visit.

In front of the church lay a field the size of a football pitch with hundreds, perhaps thousands, of small wooden crosses. At first, I thought this is what they had brought me to see but the soldier came and unlocked the school compound, which stood next to the church. He opened the old metal gate just enough to pass through and waved me in with his gun.

I had been to many African schools before but this one was eerily silent. There was no birdsong. The usual sound of children playing or reciting their lessons was missing. As I approached the first classroom, I saw why. The room was knee-deep in dead bodies. Adults and children. Decapitated skulls lay apart from their bodies. Bloodstained walls where infant heads had been dashed. In every room in that school skeletons, still wearing their clothes, lay where they had fallen in April 1994.

Today was Saturday. In the morning I would be speaking in a church in the capital city, Kigali. What message of hope could I bring to these deeply wounded people? As I stood in that room of death, almost hearing the screams of the fallen, I heard, in my spirit, a still, small voice that rang with a familiar authority. "I am the Resurrection and the Life!" The genocide was not the last word on Rwanda.

We moved with quiet respect from room to room, around the quadrangle. My heart pounded in

my chest. The scene was repeated in every room
– a vision of hell and death. Cups and plates littered
the scene. These people had been on a journey.
Believing they would escape across the border into
Tanzania, they had brought a few belongings. But
their journey, as their life, had been cut short.

After an hour or so of reflection and tears, we
said farewell to the villagers and climbed into the
army truck to begin the long and torturous route
down the mountain. As we descended, darkness
fell across the land. The mountains sat silhouetted
against the clear, starlit sky. When we reached the
main road, we were stopped by some soldiers at a
checkpoint. We should have turned left to the place
where we had left our car but the soldiers insisted
we turn right. We were now driving through the
dark African night and I had no idea what was
happening. Charles reassured me everything was
all right. We turned off the road at the first town and
the soldiers took us through the darkness into a bar.
The obligatory African power cut was in progress
but in the corner of the bar, at a table, in the glow of
a small oil lamp, sat the army major we had met that
morning. A large, serious man, he sat dressed in his
fatigues and stared at me.

"So, you have seen the bodies of our people?
What is your comment on that?" he demanded.

I was still trying to process what I had seen.

"I have never seen anything like it," I said. "The
nearest thing we had in Europe was Hitler..."

"No!" he interrupted. "Hitler was slow! He took years to kill. But these people were killed in three months. All of them."

He told me of many atrocities carried out by the killers. Many women were raped by the killers who told them, "We will not kill you now but you will die because we have AIDS and have just infected you."

Eventually, we were led out of the bar, through the darkness, to our car which a soldier had retrieved for us. We said our farewells and drove into the pitch-black night on the long journey back to the capital. At each village we were stopped by soldiers at various roadblocks and documents were checked. As we came to the village of Kayonza, Charles asked the driver to stop. He smiled and asked Adam and me to go with him into the village.

"I want to show you something," he said. It was getting late but we followed him through the darkness. We came to a small African house and he banged on the door. There was a muffled conversation with the people inside. The door was opened and we went in and sat down. By the yellow glow of a small oil lamp, I could make out an elderly couple and several youths.

"This is my Dad and my Mum," Charles said, pointing to the couple.

We had some conversation through Charles' interpretation and greeted each other. I realised I was seeing a side of Africa that no tourist was likely to see. After this short visit we returned to the car and drove through the darkness back to Kigali.

We arrived at the convent where we were staying and went to our rooms. The rooms were small but functional. A bed and a small table and chair stood on the cement floor. The door was made from steel and had a large gap at the bottom. I rolled up a towel and placed it at the bottom of the door to prevent large insects visiting me in the night. I climbed into bed and tucked the mosquito net into the mattress. By the light of a small torch, I read some scriptures and thought about tomorrow. What would I say to the people in church? As I switched off the torch, the faces of the dead seemed to emerge from the shadows in the room. I decided I was not going to have nightmares but would sleep in peace. It was not the first time dark spirits had tried to disturb me in Africa.

I sat up and said aloud, "I bind every spirit of darkness that wants to disturb me tonight. In the name of Jesus, I claim a quiet mind. I shall not have nightmares but sleep in peace. I am covered by the blood of Jesus and fully protected by him. You have no authority over me and I command you to leave me alone in Jesus' name. Amen!"

Peace came immediately and the dark visions receded. As I lay in the quietness, I wondered about the events that had brought me to Rwanda. What a strange thing for someone born in the back streets of Manchester to be in Rwanda, let alone to be preparing to speak to thousands of Rwandans about their national grief.

Chapter 2

The exploding sausage and the broken record

"It's a boy!" These were not the words my mother wanted to hear. She had only wanted a girl and now I had arrived, she had three boys. When my two younger brothers arrived some years later, my Mum admitted defeat and put her all into bringing up five boys.

I arrived, slightly startled, into the front bedroom of 27 Donleigh Street in Manchester, on 4 April 1957. In the shadow of Lancashire's 'dark satanic mills', stood row upon row of back-to-back terraced houses. Donleigh Street predated most of this housing, being the old mill workers' houses from a time when cotton was king. This unadopted road had been missed when tarmac was being laid on roads. In the constant Manchester rain, the street often turned into a quagmire and we had to help push the milk float, and other victims, out of a rut.

My Dad was a supervisor with the Royal Mail at Manchester's main sorting office and my Gran was a post lady. My Mum had worked in the telegram office when she was younger. We were people who delivered messages – an interesting start for someone who would later take a message around the world.

Perhaps my earliest memory is when lightning

struck our house, when I was about three years old. A bright flash and a loud bang interrupted breakfast. The chimney collapsed and arrived in the fireplace, sending a large plume of soot into the room. My Dad used our washing line to cordon off the street to protect passers-by from falling masonry. We were all evacuated down the street to my Gran's house to finish our breakfast, which now tasted of soot. I grew to be a skinny little boy, very fussy about food and for years would only eat cornflakes or rice pudding.

Brookdale Park stands adjacent to Donleigh Street and it was there that my friends and I lived out most of our adventures, playing cowboys and indians and, later on, war games in the woods and dells of the park. In winter the park was often transformed into an icy adventure playground. When thick fog came, we played hide and seek and often didn't find each other for hours. Summertime saw jumpers for goal posts and sticks for wickets and many arguments with referees and umpires.

As the swinging Sixties unfolded, I lived out my life there, at Donleigh Street, amid the noisy and chaotic desperation of our largely male family, for sixteen years.

My early school days, at All Saints Church of England Primary School, were relatively peaceful. Halfway through my years there, the school was transferred to a new building, as the old building, on the opposite side of the church, became a warehouse and was later demolished. In the government slum clearance programme, most of the area we lived in was pulled down. Mile after mile looked like a war zone as street after street was reduced to rubble.

We used to have one day a year when we visited the Roman Catholic Christ the King primary school to foster good relations between Protestants and Catholics. This usually amounted to the teachers having tea and cakes in the staff room while we were threatened by the Catholic kids for being protestant infidels.

It was during these primary school years that I attended an annual event known as 'C.C.C.' – Children's Christian Crusade. This was a Christian club for primary school children which ran for a week every year. I remember crowds of kids all packed into the dingy old hall known as the 'Ragged School' on Queen Street.

We were supposed to invite our friends, as the highlight of the night was to see the record broken – literally. If there were more children than the previous night, the lady who ran the club would actually break an old 78 record with a hammer. But this only happened if we helped 'break the record' of attendance. We also won prizes for everything from attendance to answering questions. I never quite understood the 'Christian' aspect of all this. I just wanted to see a woman breaking records with a hammer and get the free pencils and stuff.

Our school was right next door to the Anglican Church of All Saints, Newton Heath and had obvious links. As a result, the Rector, John Titterington, or the Curate, Raymond Cooke, would occasionally take our school assembly. The only thing I remember about those occasions was that John Titterington's shoes used to squeak as he walked on the polished hall floor. Ray Cooke once gave us all a prayer card with the Lord's Prayer in modern English – a revolution at the time.

Sometimes we had occasion to visit the church building for a service. I think there was at least an annual school service – perhaps on All Saints' day. I was also in the Cubs for a season and this meant monthly church parade. I recall the hushed presence in the church. Everyone whispered. Perhaps they didn't want God to wake up, I thought. There was a distinct smell of musty old prayer books. We were ushered into the dark pews and told to kneel down. Who were we hiding from? I never saw God in that church but I thought he was hiding somewhere near the east end of the church because only the vicars were allowed down there.

The service was based on the green 1926 prayer book and all I can recollect, these years later, is saying the creed, which told us what we believed. After the service, as we left in the same hushed tones, I noticed a large plaque on the church wall with a long list of names on it. It said these were the names of those who had 'died in the services'. I wondered if it was the morning or the evening services. Perhaps that's why everyone seemed afraid while they were in church.

Several years later, when I was about eleven

years old, a couple of friends and I decided to
attend something similar to a Children's Christian
Crusade, at a new little Pentecostal mission hall
called 'Evangel', in a back street near the Oldham
Road. There were games and quizzes just like before
but there was something different here. Towards the
end of the club, a man stood up and told us about
heaven and hell. He said that we would be going to
one or the other and that the only way to heaven was
by asking Jesus to come and live in our hearts. If we
wanted to do that, we were to stay behind at the end
and he would lead us in a prayer.

We decided to stay behind and pray the prayer.
Well, we didn't want to go to hell, did we? When the
other kids had gone and his associates were packing
up, the leader got us together and explained that if
we really believe that Jesus comes into our hearts
when we ask him, he will. We closed our eyes and
repeated the prayer, saying we were sorry for our
sins and asked God's forgiveness. We asked Jesus
to come into our hearts. As I said those words, I
really believed that Jesus came into my heart, just
like the man said.

When we finished praying, he told us that we
should all come to church every Sunday. "Oh no!"
I thought. "It's just about getting people to go to
his church! What a fool I'd been, believing all that
stuff!" I never went near the place again for years.

Those were fairly sheltered days of childhood.
Even so, there were also some disturbing moments.
When I heard about my friend's sister who had

fallen through the ice on the canal and drowned, just days after I had walked across the same canal, on the ice, and heard the thin ice in the middle of the canal begin to creak and split as I walked over it. There were days when older boys took us captive in the park, stole things from us and bullied us. There were times when my little brothers were bitten in the face by next door's dog. But all in all childhood, so far, had been a sheltered and generally bright experience. In my false optimism, I hadn't seen the dark clouds approaching on the horizon.

At the end of the last term at All Saints, we had a leavers' assembly and our headmaster and teachers wished us well. I hadn't really given it too much thought and many of us left that day with eyes a little moist and feeling a bit emotional. It was as if the security we had established over the years, was being taken from us by events beyond our control. But now the six weeks holidays were here and that was always good. Long days of doing nothing in the park and freedom from school.

The holidays were over all too quickly and I was whisked off to Moston, to the school uniform shop. Unlike primary school, high school uniform had to be worn every day. Little did I know but this was to be the least of my worries.

The fateful day came when the short walk to school was replaced by a long bus journey. I arrived at the bus stop in my ill-fitting uniform unconvinced by my parents' reassurance, "You'll grow into it." I did have my two older brothers at the same school but they didn't want to be associated with me on the bus journey, and they were at the Upper School rather that the Lower School I would be attending, as a first year pupil. The bus was packed full of rowdy teenagers, mainly boys, on the half hour journey to North Manchester High School for boys, in Moston. The school was formerly two schools – a grammar school and a secondary modern that had been amalgamated into a comprehensive school. This was my first day of being 'incomprehensive'.

I arrived at school feeling very nervous and was immediately met by two boys from the second year who called me 'Fag' and threatened to inflict every indignity they had suffered a year earlier. They informed me that they would make my life hell just for laughs. It was on this happy note that four years of hell began.

The place felt like a prison and smelt much the same. One of my older brothers was stabbed in the stomach during a disagreement on the playing field. He survived, after having stitches at the hospital. Many of the boys carried weapons such as knives and knuckledusters. Routine torture was carried out on us lesser mortals at any opportunity. Things degenerated when I was moved up two classes and then later went to the Upper School. This made Lower School seem like a picnic. Perhaps some of the worst excesses should never be put into print, but I can tell you that a boy was made handicapped when his wrists were broken for a laugh. One boy defecated in the corner of a room despite there being ample toilet facilities. There seemed no end to the depravity. In the playground, boys would suddenly thump you in the stomach just for fun.

A significant day came when we had to give a short talk in the English class, on any subject. I was painfully shy and could never have talked in front of the class. I avoided the lesson. I knew that, whatever happened in life, I would never stand in front of a group of people and talk. I just couldn't do it.

At the end of the fourth year, I could have stayed on at school – I was in the last year when you could leave school at fifteen years old. I had done well, particularly in Physics, coming first in classwork and exams for the last two years. However, the constant fighting and abuse had taken its toll and I decided to escape this hellish episode of my life for my own sanity.

I left school with no qualifications. I had low self-esteem and no ambition whatsoever. My Dad urged me to get any job I could find and then work up from there. And so I began work at a mini-market on Old Church Street in Newton Heath, at the rate of seven pounds a week. I started on the greengrocery side of things. Early mornings started with chopping the heads off London lettuce, stacking tomatoes and then filling shelves. Having been trained for five minutes on how to use the till, I was left to checkout customers on my own. Maths not being my strong point, the money in the till was often over or under what it should have been at the end of the day. This always endeared me to Mr Smith, the tyrant who owned the store.

I was moved over to the butchery counter which was good as I'd always wanted to work with animals. My first job was stuffing the heads of pigs through the mincer to sell as pet food. On another occasion, I was shown how to use the hand-cranked sausage machine and told to make sure there were no air pockets in the sausage mixture as this would cause an explosion when the machine was cranked. I duly stuffed the mixture into the sausage machine, paying scant attention to air pockets. I put the sausage skin on the nozzle and began turning the handle as instructed. The long sausage began to emerge from the machine, nicely taking up the sausage skin. Suddenly, halfway through the process there was a loud explosion and I was covered, head to foot, along with most of the room, in fresh sausage meat. Maybe that's why they call them 'bangers'.

I continued to demonstrate my flair in the retail trade but Mr Smith just never seemed impressed. For some reason, six months later, probably about the time I dropped a side of beef I was unloading from a lorry, into a muddy puddle, I was inexplicably fired on the spot. There's just no pleasing some people.

I went on to be a 'van driver's mate' at a blanket factory for six months and then went to work with my cousin at Freedman Displays – an exhibition and display company. Most of the time was spent in the workshop in Chadderton, near Oldham, building the exhibitions. Occasionally, we travelled out to reconstruct the exhibition at various sites in London like Olympia and Earls Court. It was through this job that I first travelled to London, during the boat show, where we had to build twelve stands.

I'm not sure if my cousin had discussed my appointment with the boss, Mr Freedman. But I was taken on at a very low wage of ten pounds a week. That probably sounds very low because it was. But it was also a few pounds more than what I had been earning. However, it was well below the union agreed wage. I was instructed by my cousin that the union was very active and would almost certainly ask me if I was receiving the 'going rate' during the boat show. I was told to say yes.

Sadly, my cousin didn't tell me what the going rate was. So, in the middle of constructing the exhibition, I was approached by a union official who asked me if I was receiving the 'going rate'. "Yes I am." I said with confidence, as instructed.

"And what is the going rate?" asked the union official. I blushed.

"Oo. I don't know." I said.

"What d'you mean you don't know?" he replied.

Long pause. "Are you in the union?" he asked.

"No." I admitted.

"You're not in the ******* union!?" he shouted. He stormed off and the whole of Earl's Court was brought to a standstill. Mr Freedman was summoned. After half a day of negotiations, work resumed.

I was not 'flavour of the month' but on the other hand, I had played the game but never received the 'going rate' despite becoming a member of the union. Once the exhibition was built, we hung around in London for a couple of nights until it came time to dismantle the thing and take it back to Manchester. During the day I went to see the main sights of London – Parliament, Buckingham Palace and Trafalgar Square. In the evening, the men I worked with decided we should go down to Soho and see a darker side of life. A seedy adventure into darkness.

Back home, my father had received a compulsory purchase order for our house and was informed that it was to be demolished as part of the slum clearance. I think it was this event which brought great pressure on him, as he later had a complete nervous breakdown as a result. It was also about this time that my mother began drinking heavily.

We were eventually moved onto an old council estate on the other side of the park. Further disruption came when the council decided to renovate our new home while we were still living there. There was chaos for months, with builders knocking down walls, and floorboards being ripped up to install central heating.

One afternoon, I cycled across the park to buy a newspaper. On my way back, I stopped at our old house as I saw the demolition squad move in to demolish my childhood home. I shouldn't have watched but I was like a rabbit trapped in the headlights of an oncoming vehicle. I stood at the graveside of my childhood, as the house I had grown up in was reduced to rubble. I carry the pain of that moment to this day. It was a disturbing event, perhaps never considered by the politicians keen to build the new tower blocks that they believed would solve Manchester's housing problems. The very tower blocks that have themselves now been demolished to make way for houses.

The slow daily grind continued and, despite all the disruptions and our growing dysfunction as a family, we had to get on with life.

"For here we do not have an enduring city, but we are looking for the city that is to come."
(Hebrews 13:14)

A highlight of my time at Freedman Displays was an exhibition we did in Dublin. There was great excitement in the workshop as we planned a couple of days in Ireland while the event was on. The day came and we saw the exhibition loaded into a container and leave Oldham for the journey to Dublin. Moments later my cousin, Gordon, who I worked with, discovered that we had forgotten to load the dimmer unit, which worked the spotlights, into the container. As there was increased tension with Ireland and the IRA, Gordon suggested that the dimmer unit, which bore some resemblance to a bomb detonation device, should be carried in my luggage. A few days later we were on the Aer

Lingus flight to Dublin. Fortunately, the dimmer unit was not detected and I was spared arrest. When we arrived in Dublin and started looking for a cheap guest-house in the town centre, it began to rain. I put on my fluorescent orange kagoul, at which point Gordon mentioned that orange was, historically, not a good colour to wear in the centre of Dublin. We found somewhere to stay and dropped our bags. Then we made our way to the large hotel where the exhibition was due to arrive the following day. All seemed in hand and we rested after a visit to the chip shop. Two days later, while the exhibition was on, our boss took us out into the Irish countryside and we had lunch in view of breathtaking mountains and lakes.

After two years of building exhibitions, I heard of a factory job that paid three times what I was earning, so I applied for a job there. This led to two years of monotonous, mind-numbing jobs, producing electrical components. I had no ambition or direction in my life but all that was about to change.

Chapter 3

Brian, the witch and the wardrobe

It was a warm summer evening. In the corridors of Brookdale Park School, on a youth club night, I met Brian Wright. He stood smiling, undisturbed by the shouts from the table tennis room, the loud music from the disco or the general cacophony of teenagers enjoying themselves. He was wearing a denim jacket and jeans, possibly in an attempt to build a bridge to people significantly younger than he was. Brian had that skill, that many youth workers possess, of being able to befriend young strangers and build relationships. He engaged us in the debates and issues of the day and generally spent time with my friends and me.

As we got to know him, Brian helped us engage with the community. He set up weekly visits to a children's hospital psychiatric ward. Here we played with the kids who had various types of mental illness. We built up relationships with some of the long-term patients and always came away thankful that our own lives seemed very stable and secure by comparison. Brian also introduced us to a drug rehabilitation project in the centre of Manchester. At that time, I was very ignorant about the existence or the effects of drug abuse. I saw people there who were only slightly older than me, who had become empty shells of human existence, completely unable to deal with even the basic demands of daily life. It showed me the full horror of drug abuse, which later became so widespread, and it sealed my decision at an early age to stay away from such things.

It was possibly through Brian's friendship and recommendation that three friends and I became members of staff at the youth club sometime later. After the club closed at ten o' clock, we sometimes debriefed in a local pub. It was there in the Nelson Tavern, on Lord Lane, one evening, during a natural pause in conversation, that Brian said, "Isn't Jesus wonderful?"

It was a conversation stopper and yet I was intrigued. He told us how, at church last Sunday the Rector had gathered a few people to pray for a lady who had Parkinson's disease and a few days later she was completely clear of the illness. It sounded amazing – that God might be alive and healing people today. The conversation eventually moved on to something else but I wondered in my heart about what sort of church this was. I decided that one day, when I got round to it, I would visit Brian's church and have a look for myself.

As time went on, the four 'amigos' – Pete, Roy, Eric and myself – travelled across the city to a different youth club, situated in the old Jewish quarter of Manchester, in the shadow of Victoria Railway Station. Here, among the mainly derelict synagogues of Cheetham Hill Road, stood Noel Timpson's Youth Club. This was a much busier youth club than Brookdale and offered more activities. At its heart was a subtly lit coffee bar complete with a cappuccino machine and tuck shop.

It was a dark, wet evening in late October. Outside the youth club, the streets were cloaked in the constant Manchester drizzle. As I walked placidly amid the noise and haste of the club, I couldn't help noticing Eve, a member of staff. She was very attractive. Her dark, mysterious eyes looked out from under her dark, shiny hair which framed her beautiful face. She normally wore black clothes and perfect make-up. She was one of those women who seemed too beautiful to approach. Her presence in a room drew my gaze like a magnet. Imagine my intrigue and fascination when Eve joined a few of us in the pub one evening, after the club had closed.

Just a few doors away from Noel Timpson stood The Knowlesley Hotel. An old Victorian building with high ceilings and peeling wallpaper. It was a rendezvous for all the flotsam and jetsam of that part of Manchester, attempting to drown their sorrows in alcohol. In the thick blue haze of cigarette smoke, a man dressed as a woman stood at the bar. Two ugly sisters were busy taking men upstairs for 'brief meetings'. A pair of drunken Irishmen loudly slurred an old song in the corner, competing with the juke box. Into this colourful scene we came, about a dozen of us and Eve. Policing the youth club was often a tense time and the relief that the evening was over now showed. We drank and some smoked. We laughed and competed for control of the conversation. We were busy doing nothing yet earnestly searching for personal meaning. As we poured out of the Knowlesley into the swirling Manchester drizzle, a few of us were offered a lift by Dave, one of the gang. Dave had a Morris Minor van and once we had rearranged his plumbing tools, we were able to pile into the back of the van for a lift home. As we did, Eve invited us all back to her house for coffee. As Dave steered us through the pools of orange street light and the wet Manchester traffic, Eve and I discovered we had the same birthday although, unbelievably to me, she was fifteen years older than me. She seemed a lot younger to my inexperienced eyes. We arrived at a row of back-to-back terraced houses.

Probably to the dismay of Eve's husband, who had, until now, been enjoying a quiet night baby-sitting their young daughter, we spilled into their home. The laughter and conversation continued, though more subdued, as Eve's husband retired for the night. In Eve's deep-purple sitting room, we learnt that she had grown up in Nelson, in Lancashire, in view of Pendle Hill – infamous for witchcraft and meetings of covens. Eve had developed an interest in the occult from being quite young. This may have explained the witch's broomstick that sat on top of the bookcase in the front room. We talked of ghosts, of spirits, of darkness – like children round their first camp-fire.

As two o'clock came and went, Dave was ready to go home. But others wanted to stay and talk more.

Most of the group took advantage of Dave's offer of a lift home but three of us stayed for more coffee and chat. The last bus had long gone and the day was far spent. Eve suggested the three of us should stay and sleep on the floor. The others declined and decided to walk several miles home but, curious about this new world I was discovering, I accepted the offer. The others bid farewell and disappeared into the night. Eve went upstairs and returned with some blankets. She said good night and then, suddenly, and certainly unexpectedly, she embraced me and kissed me passionately. It took me by surprise but it was very pleasant and yet disturbing. She left without comment and went to bed. As I lay on the sofa and put out the light, the room was bathed in moonlight from a full moon framed in the skylight.

I pondered on the night. This beautiful female. Her mysterious glances in my direction, the flash of her smile, her acceptance, the passionate embrace, the kiss. It had all stirred my heart. Was this the love I had been looking for? It felt so powerful, so satisfying and yet left me wanting more, much more. But what of her husband, her daughter? How did all that fit in? I drifted into a fitful sleep for a few hours before leaving very early for work. I longed for my next meeting with Eve.

Sometime later, I was sitting with Brian Wright in the Nelson Tavern. I was bemoaning that fact that at home, there was always noise. With four brothers and living in an urban area, there was always noise.

I greatly valued solitude, silence and space to think. Brian said he was going to a very quiet place in a couple of weeks time. He was going to visit a monastery for a weekend retreat. There would be complete silence up to lunchtime every day. He offered to investigate if it would be possible for me to join him. I was unsure about the idea but thought it would be good to have a quiet adventure.

So it was that Brian and I set off in his car a few weeks later, crossing the Pennines in thick, swirling fog. After a couple of hours, we arrived at the Community of the Resurrection in Mirfield, West Yorkshire. Brian's contact was Hugh Whistler, a gentle old man who was full of the Holy Spirit. They had arranged to visit a healing service over the weekend and to talk about something called the 'charismatic movement'. It sounded like a part of a washing machine to me. After settling into our rooms we went for supper with the brothers, which all seemed terribly upper class to this boy from the slums. The day ended with the service of Compline, which I was quite sure was a bedtime drink. In the shadows of the community chapel, I sat with Brian and listened to the soothing plainsong of the brothers and the chanting of Psalm 91, a psalm of God's protection.

It was a peaceful end to the day and the silence started as the service finished. We walked quietly through the dimly lit corridors back to our rooms. No TV or radio. No loud conversations. Just silence and a simple room with bed, table and chair. I was so unused to the silence I had trouble falling to sleep. I looked at the crucifix on the wall and wondered about Jesus. I fell asleep and had several strange dreams but a silent night. Holy night.

Before breakfast, Brian and I walked round the vast grounds of the monastery. At one edge of the estate there is a boundary wall and the land falls away steeply from there, giving breathtaking views of the surrounding hills. We also walked past the life-size crucifix in the Calvary garden, then back to the house. Breakfast was in silence – a first for me. Afterwards, Brian went to the morning service but I returned to my room to enjoy the silence. After a few minutes of pondering this unusual experience, I noticed a large Bible on the table. I'd never really read the Bible before. I had read the first few chapters of Genesis but always got bogged down during the outbreak of 'begetting' that happens in Genesis chapter five. Not really sure what 'begetting' was, it was all a little confusing. This time, however, I opened the Bible in the New Testament. I had no idea what I would find. I glanced randomly at the page and read these words.

"A voice was heard in Ramah,
Lamentation, weeping, and great mourning,
Rachel weeping for her children,
Refusing to be comforted,
Because they are no more."
(Matthew 2:18)

I read the words a second time. I began weeping uncontrollably. Deep sobbing, as though this Rachel,

I had never heard of, was very close to me. I heard the screams of children in my heart. The weeping of their mothers. I closed the book and lay on the bed. What was that about? Why did that powerful emotion come upon me just now? Little did I know then that I would one day look into the eyes of Rachel and enter deeply into her mourning.

I returned to Mirfield on several occasions and found time to think about life and its purpose. I bought a copy of J. B. Phillips' translation of the New Testament which was written in plain English. The story of Jesus unfolded before me as never before as, over several months, I read all four gospels and the Acts of the Apostles as I sat at work during lunchtime. J. B. Phillips once said that, when he was translating the Bible, it was like "rewiring a house with the electricity switched on". In many ways, I had a similar experience as I read the New Testament in a language I could understand for the first time. I read it through like a novel or a biography, rather than as a sacred text. It introduced me to Jesus in a deep way. The purity of the scriptures stood in stark contrast to the depravity and chaos of my own life.

Jim + Eve

A kiss late one night had developed into a strange affair between Eve and me. We were rarely alone but something had developed between us that was more than physical. There was a strange spiritual force that surprised us both. Eve was taking a huge risk with her marriage and family but we tried not to think about that and both lived for any moment we could be together, even if not alone.

The conversations about the occult had continued and came to a head when Eve suggested we should have a seance at her home. One Saturday night we met at her house with a few friends and Eve's husband Andrew. Nothing happened until Eve and I were the only ones left at the table. Then it appeared there was a message from "S–A–T–A–N" for someone called "E–G–A–N" and the message was "D–E–A–T–H". That brought matters to an end and all concerned thought we should stop. But where did that leave me? What had happened? Was it real and was I in danger? Eve seemed out of her depth but did try to reassure me things would be all right.

I was more interested in the relationship with her than the occult and dreamed of the day we could finally be together. Friends had been warning me I was playing with fire and it would all end in tears. However, love is blind and I wouldn't listen. I am so grateful that a friend moved behind the scenes and sent a friend of Eve's to visit her and face her with the truth of what she was doing. The next time we met, Eve made it plain that the relationship was over but we could still be friends. To say I was devastated would be an understatement. I couldn't imagine happiness without her. Life seemed to be over. It wasn't, of course. What I hadn't realised was that there had been a battle for my soul. Brian and Eve were the physical manifestation of the battle warring in the spiritual realms. Brian had been used to lead me to the light of Jesus and Eve used to drive me into darkness. /

A few weeks later I woke early on a Sunday. This was very unusual for me. I rarely surfaced before noon on a Sunday. In the distance I heard the bells from a church somewhere on the 'new estate'. I had heard them every Sunday for ten years and always dozed back to sleep. On this day, though, I felt wide-awake. A thought came to me as I lay there. I could visit Brian's church. I'd meant to for ages and never got round to it. I got dressed and rushed out of the door. If I hurried I could just get there in time. I took a short cut across the park and through Paddock Lane School. The school gates were locked so I climbed over the fence into Paddock Lane. Those bells were still ringing and were getting louder. As I arrived at the church, I was surprised to find that this is where the bells were. I had heard these bells for all these years and never knew where they were. I arrived breathless at the door of Holy Family Church on Lord Lane. A man gave me a collection of books and welcomed me in. Brian wasn't there so I found a seat and sat down. When Brian arrived I moved and sat with him.

As the service began, I noticed that some people were doing more than singing hymns. Some raised their hands and faces towards the mosaic of the risen Jesus at the front of the church but they were seeing something beyond it. There was electricity in the air. As they sang, I closed my eyes and said under my breath, "Jesus, if you are there, come into my life." I was immediately aware of how dirty I was inside. I didn't know the doctrine of original sin at that time but, in my heart, I now experienced my sin. I was going to run out of the church, I felt so uncomfortable. Then, almost immediately, I felt like I was standing under a waterfall of pure warm water. A warm shower of living water was washing me clean on the inside. Every last stain was gone. I was filled with a light brighter than the sun. A joy and happiness I had never known welled up inside. Then somewhere deep inside I heard a small voice. "I did come into your life when you asked me to as a child. I have been with you all this time. It is you who have been ignoring me." I saw now that, there in that children's club, in the Pentecostal church, years ago, I had asked Jesus to come into my heart and he had. But I had neglected him. I was shown countless occasions from my past – desperate situations when I had cried out to God. He had always saved me and I had gone on without a word of thanks, ignoring him until the next crisis. Now, the Jesus I had read of in that New Testament stood inside me – or was I in him, or both? Above all, I suddenly knew I was loved – completely and unconditionally.

In one of C. S. Lewis' stories, a little girl called Lucy, exploring an old house, finds a large wardrobe full of coats. She climbs in and tries to find the back of the wardrobe but she finds herself slipping into another world she didn't know existed. A fascinating story unfolds. That day, when I went to church, I slipped into another world I didn't know existed. I was transferred from the kingdom of darkness into the kingdom of light. I had slipped through the wardrobe into a new world. The prodigal had come home.

Jesus said, "I am the door. If anyone enters by me, he will be saved, and will go in and out and find pasture."

(John 10:9)

Chapter 4

The girl, the circus tent and the Holy Family

Spring was in the air. Lambs appeared on the hills. Fluffy ducklings followed their mothers in procession. At Noel Timpson's Youth Centre teenagers were pairing off at an alarming rate. It was in this frenzy of newly forming couples that I overcame my painful shyness and asked an equally shy young lady to go out with me. We were so nervous it almost didn't happen.

Hazel and I began a simple courtship. We had little in common and it is a miracle the relationship lasted. We began doing all the normal things young couples do – mainly just spending time together. In fact, we couldn't face being apart, so much so that I virtually moved into her parents' house, sleeping on the couch most nights. We did spend many nights at the youth club as we were both employed there in the evenings. Hazel ran the coffee bar and I would always find an excuse to hang around there with her, when I could.

It was a few months after we had begun our relationship, when I had the encounter with God at Holy Family Church and became a Christian. This began to cause some friction between us as Hazel really didn't want to get involved at church or 'get religion'. Jesus had become so important to me that I couldn't imagine being with someone who wasn't a Christian. I couldn't imagine being without Hazel either. So I began to pray that she would have an encounter with Jesus too. To this day, I don't think I have ever invested so much time in prayer for one thing as I did in praying for Hazel to know Jesus.

As the weeks went by, I attended Holy Family every Sunday. I discovered that the church had actually started down the road in a pub. As the estate was being built, All Saints Church had decided to plant a church on the new estate. Ray Cooke, now the rector of Holy Family, had obtained permission to hold services in the lounge bar of the Nelson Tavern. An altar cloth was draped over the bar for communion services. This had been the place where Brian Wright first told me about Jesus being alive today. It seemed the work of the church had continued in the pub even after the church had moved into its newly built premises further up the road.

At the church, a lady called Lilian Bradshaw and her husband Jim began to encourage me and we became good friends. Another couple, Keith and Myra Ashworth, also invested godly counsel into my life. Keith and Myra were, in many respects, unlikely people to find at the Anglo-catholic church of Holy Family, being evangelicals and previously not even Anglican. Their love and reverence of the scriptures fed my spirit and rubbed off on me a great deal. In truth, the whole family of the church welcomed me warmly.

Shortly after becoming a Christian I lost my job.

I'd been working as a leader in a youth and sports club in Manchester city centre. Unemployment had reached one million for the first time and Jim Callahan's government seemed unable to stop it rising further. One day I was at the job centre looking for work. When I came out I discovered my bicycle had been stolen. It was a great loss because I cycled everywhere. So began a whole year without work. I went to the job centre several times a week and applied for everything available but to no avail. What I did do during that time was to pray and spend time worshipping God. Though life was hard, God gave me peace. I believed things would change for the better.

That October a circus tent came to Manchester for a week. But this was no circus. It was a 3,000 seater tent owned by an evangelist called David Sherman. His pentecostal team came and worked with local churches to reach the area with the gospel of Jesus. I attended most nights with my Dad. He had overcome his breakdown when, late one night, he had read the Beatitudes in the Bible and had his own encounter with Jesus. He was a changed man and soon after became a church warden at Holy Family. For weeks he was known at church as 'Don's Dad' but gradually people came to know him as Peter, a faithful, unassuming servant of God and others.

I was impressed by the impact these tent evangelists were having on the area and the whole way they preached a clear message and saw people giving their lives to Jesus every night. In my heart,

I thought, I would love to do this but it seemed only a dream.

Having watched many others come to Jesus at these meetings, I determined to get Hazel to the tent at all costs. Unfortunately, that was the last thing she wanted to do. Very reluctantly, under much pressure from me, she came to the tent. It was a wet, dark, cold night. Sitting in the tent our feet were freezing. Testimony time came and I hoped for another dazzling testimony like we had heard on previous evenings. What transpired was one of the most boring, unconvincing testimonies from a missionary couple I have ever heard. The preacher, a man called Clive, didn't impress her either, though actually, I think he spoke well. As people went forward I hoped Hazel would go with them. But she was furious that I had dragged her to this freezing cold tent and made her sit through all this religion. As we parted that night, she said, "That preacher said it is not enough to know about Jesus. We have to ask him into our life. How do you do that?"

I explained that it was just as simple as asking, in a prayer, for Jesus to forgive our past and invite him to come into our heart, and promise to put him first in our life.

"Oh," she said.

I left it at that for fear of making matters worse than they were.

On the last day of the tent mission I received a letter telling me I had a job with Save the Children Fund working in Moss Side in Manchester. It was a twelve-month contract working with Childminders and small children.

A few weeks later, I asked Hazel if she had got around to asking Jesus into her life.

"Yes," she said. "Before I went to bed that night, I asked him to come in."

Slowly, over the weeks that followed, I saw a gradual change as she grew to love the Jesus I had met. We came to God in very different ways but we became part of the family at Holy Family Church and were there regularly. With the encouragement of so many people we grew in our love for God and each other.

The rector, Ray Cooke, was a great encouragement and very welcoming. During the twelve months I was unemployed he sometimes invited me for breakfast when I attended morning prayer midweek. I remembering him saying during a sermon that we need Jesus but we also need to be baptised in the Holy Spirit. I didn't know anything about that but I found a book called 'The Holy Spirit and you', by Dennis Bennett, and began to read it. Near the end of the book, there was a prayer asking for the baptism of the Holy Spirit. I went to the bathroom and knelt down by the bath. What an appropriate place, I thought. As the book suggested, I first renounced all my involvement with the occult and then I prayed for the Holy Spirit to baptise me. A quiet peace came on me and very quietly I began to speak in tongues – a new prayer language – just as the book had explained. It was very quiet and undramatic but a new power began to flow through me.

Another friend I met at Holy Family was an ex-hippy called Paul Hoyle. I am very grateful to Paul for introducing me to Billy Graham's Hour of Decision programme on the radio. In those days it was only available on Radio Luxembourg and the signal moved about, requiring the radio tuner to be constantly tweaked. There was a lot of interference but we heard many messages calling the lost to Jesus and details of the campaigns. One night we were listening to the broadcast when Billy Graham was in India. He was speaking through an interpreter. I had never heard anything like it and was greatly moved by it. I had no idea that I, too, would speak through an interpreter to explain the good news many times in years to come.

There were many other friends from those Holy Family days and most of them had some input into my life. Holy Family held occasional Days of Renewal and people came form miles around, from all over the North West and beyond, to be there. One man, who came to these days, was Captain Ian Ferguson of the Church Army. Ian, a Geordie, was one of the chaplains at Strangeways prison in Manchester and worked with Noel Procter, the senior chaplain at the prison. I was always encouraged by Ian. He was down to earth, had a certain twinkle in his eye and always seemed full of Jesus. He normally saw three or four men turn to Jesus every week in the jail. He always had fresh stories of God's miracle power. I had no idea what the Church Army was and Ian's grey uniform, which made him look like a bus conductor, meant I didn't really want to know either.

There was a tremendous move of the Holy Spirit in those days and many lives were touched by God. Many came to know the Lord and many people were healed at Holy Family. On Thursday evenings a small group of us met in a room at the church for worship, prayer and Bible teaching. The Holy Spirit was powerfully present and manifested the gifts of the Holy Spirit. Many were called out into ministry from that church family – some to the priesthood, some to pioneer new work and several evangelists.

I had a growing love for Jesus yet I was still very shy. I had taken to wearing a large cross in those days. The shyness and the passion for Jesus were heading for a collision. One day, shortly after I started work with Save the Children, a colleague asked me why I wore the cross. It took me by surprise and I am ashamed to say that I said there was no particular reason. Immediately, I felt God's disappointment. I had denied him and let him down. I prayed that God would give me a second chance. The very next day, another colleague, a keen feminist, asked the exact same question. "Why do you wear that cross?"

"Oh, it's a long story," I said.

"I've got plenty of time," she said.

I told her I was a Christian and she told me that when her father had been dying, she had prayed to

God to save him but he died.

"I don't know about that," I said. "All I know, is that Jesus died for me and I want to live for him."

A Jewish lady joined the conversation. "Why do Christians always say to me, 'You killed our Lord'?" she asked.

"I don't know about that," I said. "All I know, is that Jesus died for me and I want to live for him."

Soon about eight people were firing questions about God at me. I repeated my mantra. "I don't know about that. All I know, is that Jesus died for me and I want to live for him."

At the end of the evening the first lady said to me, "You have really made me think tonight."

What I noticed was that when I began to stand up for Jesus, I felt his power right there with me. It didn't come until I began to speak but it came as soon as I began the first sentence. I grew in my desire to tell people about this wonderful Jesus who, I knew, could change their life.

I think I really 'caught' evangelism from listening to the Billy Graham radio broadcast. I knew that several people who attended church had not committed their life to Christ. I knew this through personal conversations with them. A growing urgency began to grow in me to call people to receive Jesus. Through the gracious encouragement of Ray Cooke, I began preaching occasionally on Sunday mornings at Holy Family. I usually ended with a call to receive Jesus as Saviour. Some people mocked me as a 'fundamentalist' and called me 'the Billy Graham of Failsworth' but I took both as great compliments.

Chapter 5

Call to the nations

Did I spend too much time thinking? Possibly. But I had been thinking lately about my life. Did I want to spend my life driving a minibus? This is what I did for a living and I knew people in their late fifties who drove minibuses for community groups. It was clearly possible to make it a career choice.

I took a morning off one sunny day. I made some coffee and toast and opened the French windows in our second floor flat, in Manchester's bedsit land. I read my Bible and prayed and decided something. I didn't really want to drive a minibus for the rest of my life. Could God use me? I had no skill or gift, it seemed. I prayed, "Lord, I don't have much. But what I have you can have. I bring the little I have – like that little boy who offered his packed lunch to you. With his meagre offering you fed 5,000 men plus women and children and had twelve baskets left over. Lord, I don't amount to much but all that I am and have, I give to you today. I hereby give you my life. You can use me as you wish. All the years I have left, be they many or few, are yours. Take me. Break me. Use me in your service."

It was a dangerous prayer but I've never been more sincere than I was on that day. I carried that offering with me for two weeks.

The little kettle on the camping stove finally came to the boil. I made a welcome cup of coffee. I was sitting on the ground outside our tent, in a field, reading my Bible. Hazel had gone off to wash the plates. We were camping in the Lake District, at Troutbeck Bridge, near Lake Windermere. I had often camped in the Lakes with various groups of young people and smaller groups of friends. It isn't too far from Manchester and the landscape is breathtaking.

(It had been on an earlier trip to the Lakes that I walked into a bookshop in Ambleside, not realising it was a Christian bookshop. I'd found a small booklet called 'Journey into Life' by Norman Warren. It was a very clear explanation of the gospel and why we needed Jesus to save us. It clearly explained the love and justice of God and why Jesus had died on the cross. It concluded with a prayer of commitment, similar to the one I had prayed as a child. I'd sat by Lake Coniston one crisp autumn afternoon and prayed that prayer. I read the book several times afterwards and I believe it really paved the way for my encounter with Jesus at Holy Family.)

As a new Christian, I began to devour the scriptures. I'd bought a 'Living Bible' which was written in plain English. I'd just read the whole book of Isaiah, though not understood much of it. So, on this particular trip, to a campsite near Lake Windermere, I decided to begin another major Old Testament book. I turned the page and found the Book of Jeremiah. I began reading and very soon came to the verses about Jeremiah's call.

Then the word of the LORD came to me,
saying:
"Before I formed you in the womb I knew
you;
Before you were born I sanctified you;
I ordained you a prophet to the nations."

As I read those words, I had a strange experience.
The words seemed to jump off the page and I felt
the power of God come upon me. In my heart, I got
a sudden conviction that God wanted me to go to
other nations and preach the gospel. I saw myself on
a platform in front of thousands of people.

The idea seemed ridiculous. I was a minibus
driver from Manchester and just turned twenty. The
trip to Dublin had seemed the furthest I would ever
travel. Apart from anything else I was too young.
I was just a youth from the youth club! I shrugged
the idea off.

I looked down at the page and read Jeremiah's
reply.

"Ah, Sovereign LORD," I said, "I do not
know how to speak; I am only a youth."

Jeremiah had said the same thing I had just said –
"I'm too young." I think God had heard my excuse
before. I read on.

But the LORD said to me, "Do not say, 'I am
only a youth.' You must go to everyone I send

you to and say whatever I command you. Do
not be afraid of them, for I am with you and
will rescue you," declares the LORD.
Then the LORD reached out his hand and
touched my mouth and said to me, "Now, I
have put my words in your mouth.
See, today I appoint you over nations and
kingdoms to uproot and tear down, to destroy
and overthrow, to build and to plant."

There was such authority in these words and I felt
God was speaking to me. It was too much. Too far
beyond my comprehension. I looked out across the
beautiful Lakeland mountains. Majestic clouds sat
in a blue summer sky. A gentle breeze played in the
grass-covered slopes. On nearby hills sheep bleated.
I was taken aback by God. I told God that he could
take my life and use it as he wished but what he had
just shown me was beyond my comprehension.

I didn't chase this vision but I treasured these
things quietly in my heart. I recalled some weeks
earlier telling God that he could have my life, to do
with as he wished. Perhaps that had been a dangerous
prayer. Many people I know can't let go of their life.
But I had done. In all purity, a few weeks ago, I had
told God he could have my life.

Back in Manchester the year had flown by and
the job contract came to an end. By a strange quirk
of events, as most of the sixteen people who had
started work with me lost their jobs, I was chosen
to stay on, with two others, for another five years.

Hazel was now pursuing a career in social housing management and we decided the time was right to get married. We got engaged just before I lost my previous job, so our engagement had lasted over two years. We married at Holy Family on Sunday 26 August 1979. The curate, Andrew Wells, conducted the wedding and Ray Cooke preached an evangelistic sermon at my request. As I look back at the photos of that day, it looks like the annual meeting of the Hair Bear Bunch. But I'm not sure who won the prize for the most ridiculous hairstyle.

During the reception, as the disco pumped out loud music and flashing lights in the church hall, my friend John, slightly the worse for drink, said he wanted to give his life to Jesus. I suggested it might be better in the morning as he might not remember it, if we did it now. But he insisted this was the right time. We could hardly hear each other for the loud music but, in the corner of the hall, I shouted a prayer of commitment, line by line, into his ear and he shouted it back. I shouted another prayer at him and he was happy. It was a strange place to lead someone to Jesus but there is never a wrong time for that.

We moved to our first flat in Whalley Range, a rough area of Manchester near Moss Side. I think our naivety protected us as we lived there. We lived among prostitutes and drug pushers and didn't really notice. The flat was very peaceful most of the time and we were happy there.

Occasionally I visited Sharon Pentecostal church

in Moss Side. The congregation were predominately Jamaican although the Pastor, Bill Barratt, was a white man. There was a great love of the scriptures there and a faith that God moved today in healings and miracles. Looking back, I was tapping into the riches of the church at two extremes – the Anglo-catholic charismatic worship at Holy Family and the Pentecostal protestantism of Sharon. Both were a great blessing for which I am very thankful. I loved the reverence of the Anglican worship and the charismatic power. I also valued the evangelical truth and pentecostal fervour of Sharon's pentecostals. I never saw any contradiction in attending services at both churches on the same day.

The darkness of Whalley Range did eventually manifest, as our nights began to be interrupted by joyriders and fire-starters. The empty house opposite our bedroom window was set on fire several times in the early hours and the rest of the night was spent listening to fire engines and their crews trying to put out the fire. After two weeks without a night's sleep, we became desperate. At the height of the disturbances, I spent a Saturday night in prayer asking for God to stop the noise. No answer came and the disturbance continued till daybreak. I was quite angry with God for not answering my prayers.

Bleary-eyed we travelled across the city to Holy Family's morning service. I wasn't in the mood to engage with the service and was still muttering against God when Gordon Smith stood up to read the Old Testament reading. (Gordon was married to Ruth, who had been one of my primary school teachers). As Gordon read the lesson, my mouth dropped open. Was this God speaking to us again?

> "And I will provide a place for my people Israel and will plant them so that they can have a home of their own and no longer be disturbed. Wicked people will not disturb them any more, as they did at the beginning..."
>
> (1 Chronicles 17:9)

It seemed this was the answer I had sought – "I will provide a place for my people... and will plant them so that they can have a home of their own and no longer be disturbed."

I had wanted God to make the street quiet but God had bigger plans – a home of our own. Within the year we had taken out a mortgage and moved to Derbyshire Road in Newton Heath. Here, the youngest resident was in their late seventies, with the exception of a young couple who lived opposite. It was one of the quietest places we have ever lived. It was also only a short walk from Holy Family and my parents. Hazel wasn't sure about moving so far away from her parents though.

The house purchase took ages as the vendors had trouble completing on their new home. One weekend, when we should have moved, we went to the Lake District for a holiday, to take our mind off the disappointment.

The day we moved, we hired a small van and spent the day going back and forth from the flat to our new home. Eventually, most of the stuff had been moved.

I went to evensong at Holy Family the night we moved in. After the service, I was chatting to my friend Geoff Morris and boldly told him, "I'm never moving home again!"

"Don't let him hear you say that," he smiled, nodding towards the mosaic of Jesus at the front of church. Unfortunately I just had.

Chapter 6

The valley of the shadow of death

After we had settled into our new home, Hazel and I decided to start a family. About a year later, our first child, Rebecca was born. The labour had taken fourteen hours and Hazel had been in danger of losing her life during the birth. Mercifully she survived and eventually returned home with Rebecca and we started family life together. Everything seemed to be going well. As Rebecca grew, Hazel returned to work. I would drop Rebecca off at the child-minder's house on my way to work. Life was happy and fulfilling.

Then, one day I had a message that my mother had fallen and banged her head and was in hospital. I presumed the stay in hospital would be a routine few days. She was only in her fifties. However, on visiting my mother I was a little shocked by her condition. I asked to speak to a doctor to reassure myself, but the reassurance didn't come. Years of heavy drinking had taken their toll and now my mother was suffering a liver failure. I was left in no doubt that the end may be near for my mother.

I emerged from the hospital into the darkness and ran through the heavy Manchester rain back to the car. I climbed in and sat in the quietness. As the raindrops rolled down the windscreen, tears fell from my eyes. Slowly, thoughtfully, I prayed more seriously than ever before. Something deep inside impressed upon me that the end was near. With great heaviness of heart, I told God that, whatever the outcome, he would always be God. Nevertheless, I asked that he would save my mother's life at this time. I had not yet appreciated that death was God's ferocious enemy. Over the next week or so, my mother seemed to recover well. She looked a bit yellow but was in good spirits. In fact, some heaviness of recent years seemed to have lifted from her face. She seemed more like the younger mother I had known as a child. I began to relax a little. One morning the phone rang. It was my father, his voice a little shaky. "Your mother passed away in the early hours this morning." I forget the end of the conversation. Suddenly, I felt like a high-speed train had hit me. I ran upstairs and fell across the floor unable to take in the news.

No! No! No! It couldn't be true! This was the first death of anyone close to me. My spirit sank so low. I felt like someone had cut a spiritual cord. I felt so alone in the world. The one who had given me life was now dead. I felt numb with the shock for several days. Death had come like a thief in the night. As the pain eased, I hoped that things would get better.

After six years of working for Save the Children, I began to pray to God for direction and offered my life unconditionally for his use. I had a growing desire to be in full-time ministry – it dominated my waking thoughts. The only ministry I knew was the Anglican priesthood and so I began to pursue that by talking with various people. Hazel's only conditions were that she didn't want to be a vicar's wife and she did not want to be a missionary living in... 'Matabeleland'. She had no idea where that was but it became our generic term for a remote place in Africa.

It soon became clear that the priesthood was not the way forward – no one stopped me or discouraged me but, in the spirit, I felt the door close. God cannot steer a stationary car, so as I moved towards the ministry of the priesthood, God firmly turned the wheel in another direction.

There was another weekend of renewal at church and Ian Ferguson brought a display highlighting the ministry of Church Army. Church Army is an Anglican society of evangelists who work in the Church of England doing, and training others in, evangelism. Several people suggested that this ministry could be the way forward for me. I was horrified. "Over my dead body," I thought. "I'm not wearing a uniform like that!" Then Hazel started suggesting it could be the way forward too. Jesus said, "A man's enemies will be the members of his own household." (Matthew 10:36). How true that now felt!

However, God reminded me that I had offered him my life, unreservedly, for his service. I began to sense, reluctantly, that this was God's way forward. I went to see Ian Ferguson to discuss what was involved. It would mean three years training in

London and then posting to a ministry who knows where? He did tell me not to go unless Hazel was one hundred percent behind the idea, otherwise it could wreck our marriage. Wise words indeed. I was really relying on Hazel not wanting to move to London so I didn't have to go through with it. However, Hazel got this amazing peace about moving to London and making a fresh start. I had run out of excuses.

I had one more hurdle to jump – my own reluctance. I knew I stood at a crossroads. The outcome of my life stood in the balance. I had a growing fear of losing my anonymity. Once in ministry, in many ways, I would be a public figure. I wrestled for weeks about this. Then one day I went into town to look round the Christian World Bookshop on Deansgate. I found a copy of 'The Luis Palau story'. Luis Palau had once been called 'the Billy Graham of Latin America'. I had heard Luis on tapes and liked his style of evangelism. I bought the book and began reading it in the coffee bar of the bookshop. I read the first three chapters right through. It began with the story of how Luis led a hardened communist to Christ, live on the air, during one of his TV programmes that accompanied his crusades. As I read those pages, I decided that this is what I wanted to do with my life – to go on an adventure with God and see men and women give their lives to Jesus. The dramatic blessing of Jesus I had experienced, could be spread to many others.

I reluctantly applied to Church Army. After

two local interviews, Hazel and I were invited to a selection weekend at the college in Blackheath, London. We arrived on a sharp spring afternoon and walked apprehensively up the drive of the college. We approached the front door of the grand Victorian building. We were welcomed into the large hallway. An imposing portrait of Wilson Carlile, the founder, hung in the equally imposing stairway from the hall. We were welcomed into coffee as we waited for the rest of the candidates to arrive. As we mingled, we chatted to a young man who was also a candidate for selection. As we shared, I sensed we had a similar calling on our lives. We both wanted to see the lost come to know Jesus, we longed for revival in Britain and we weren't particularly bothered about the trappings of the Church. The young man's name was Kerry Dixon. During the course of the weekend we had interviews with various people and I was quite open about the fact that I didn't really want to be in Church Army but was here in obedience to God's call. We went to visit a project for the homeless run by Church Army and led a service there. We returned to Manchester and waited for the decision.

A few days later, we received the news that I had been accepted for training with Church Army. We began preparations for this life-changing decision. Hazel was now pregnant with our second child. The birth was easier and our son Philip was born at the beginning of August. Hazel and Philip came home and all seemed well until one day, as he cried, Philip went very blue. Fortunately, the nurse was visiting Hazel at our home when it happened. A doctor was called, who detected problems with Philip's heart. He was rushed to hospital where he and Hazel were kept in overnight. We spent the rest of the afternoon talking to doctors, having X-rays taken and then Philip was admitted for the night, along with Hazel.

The following day Hazel and Philip were transferred to Manchester Children's Hospital, where Philip had more tests. They decided that they should stay there and put him on a course of medicine. Hazel and I chatted with the doctor later that day and he informed us that Philip had congenital heart disease. As we were due to move to London at the end of August, the hospital arranged to transfer Philip to Great Ormond Street Hospital.

Hazel and Philip arrived in London, with a nurse escort, while I arranged the removal of our belongings and little Rebecca.

At Great Ormond Street Hospital, Philip had more tests. His consultant explained Philip's condition and that he would need heart surgery. He told us that he had a complex problem and that this operation would relieve the extra pressure that was currently on his lungs. This would be to 'band'or make narrow the artery to the lung. He had a restriction on the artery to the body and they would remove this. Besides this, two of the arteries were connected to the wrong side of his heart. He also had a hole in his heart, but he was just too small for anything to be done about these things now.

The suggested surgery was to enable him to grow big enough for further surgery to be done and to save him from respiratory failure. They asked us to think about this operation and to let the consultant know whether Philip could undergo surgery. They told us the success rate was about seventy percent. If he didn't undergo this operation, his lungs would fail him in about three months. In other words he wouldn't live to see Christmas.

They told us to take into consideration that assuming this operation was successful there would be no promise that future surgery would be successful. They could not even guarantee that anything else could be done for him. So we knew from the beginning that we risked losing Philip. It could have been while he was small or when he was older and we knew him better. We chose to give him a chance.

On 3 September he underwent his first operation. It was successful and Philip recovered very well. On 16 September they discharged him from hospital and we began our new life together as a new family in our new home in London. Philip often went to Great Ormond Street Hospital for regular check-ups. He grew, began to put on weight, cut his teeth, started crawling and did everything that any other child would do. He was still on medication which he needed to remain stable. He would often have fainting fits and turn blue, which was very disturbing but we tried our best to live a normal life.

College was a difficult time for Hazel and me. Hazel was a young mother with two small children, one of whom had to visit hospital regularly. I had a new group of friends who were all single and the new task of debating answers to theological questions that no one, in the normal world, was asking. I also had to travel away on ministry placements once a term. The sale of our house in Manchester had fallen through and this was giving us severe financial problems as we tried to pay a mortgage while living on a college bursary.

During the second year of college I received a telephone call to say that they had taken my father into hospital with cancer. We arranged to visit him in Manchester as soon as possible. On arriving at the hospital, we found my father semi-conscious and I wasn't sure if he was aware that we were even there. Hazel took the children for a walk and I looked at the shadow of the man I knew as Dad. So healthy for most of his life and impatient with illness, I realised that events were beginning to repeat themselves. He was not going to recover. As I sat by the bed holding his hand, it seemed even now, although he was breathing, that death had already stolen him away. A tear rolled down my face and onto the bed. I wanted him to wake up so I could speak to him. I knew in my heart of hearts that this would be the last time I would see him alive. As we returned to London, the same mixture of anger, defeat and loss that had accompanied the news of my mother's death, came over me like a black cloud.

It was 5.30am two weeks later. I woke to the sound of the phone ringing. "Who would be ringing at this hour?" I thought, "Unless..." It was my eldest brother with news that Dad had died a few moments before. I went back to bed and broke the news to Hazel. I sat in bed in the quiet half-light of the early morning while Hazel went downstairs to make a drink. The street was still quiet. A milk float whined by. As I sat there, no tears would come. I had cried them all after that visit to the hospital.

After a coffee, I decided to go into college early. I had never attended the early morning communion service. The college Principal looked surprised to see me as did a few of the other regulars at this optional service. It was All Souls' day, the night after Hallowe'en. All the readings and prayers were about resurrection and overcoming death. What a comfort God's promises were. We travelled to Manchester for the funeral. It was my unfortunate job to tell my Gran – my father's mother – of his death. She was now in her nineties. We returned to London and, after a period of adjustment, life had to go on. In fact, I had exams that day. Rebecca was starting school and little Philip had all his problems. Hazel, who so often faced Philip's difficulties when I was not there, takes up the story.

Philip went to hospital for another test which was very successful. He had one of his fainting attacks the day after the test while still in hospital. The nurses were quite worried about him and called the doctors. The consultant told me the night before this that they had discovered a lot of muscle growth within the heart. He said Philip should continue with his medicine and out-patients and that they would operate when he was about five.

When the doctors saw Philip having one of his attacks, they decided that the extra muscle growth was reducing the blood supply to the body. They gave him a blood transfusion and changed his drugs. He was discharged later that evening. They told me that the drugs would relax the heart muscle and that the attacks would probably stop. They planned to operate before the end of the year.

The new medicine was wonderful. Philip had a new spark about him. He ate better, slept better and was so active. He even put on weight at a quicker rate. Four days later he had an attack. This time it was different; he went blue and his breathing altered. I took him to out-patients the following day after talking to the doctor on the telephone. The consultant examined him and looked very concerned. Then he explained that Philip should have surgery before we moved in June, that the operation was very major and he was uncertain about what could be done. But he was worried about these attacks. Philip might fall asleep and never wake up. We booked another appointment for two weeks time.

Those two weeks were fabulous. Philip was happy, joyful, bright and appeared to be very healthy. He walked more, ate more and his weight increased. I believed that Philip was healed at one point because he looked so well.

On the morning of his appointment Philip became ill. He was sick and his colour changed to blue again, only this time I think he blacked out. I wrapped him up as he was cold although it was quite a mild day, and got on the train to go to the hospital. He was very still and quiet on this journey and once I had to shake him as he was so still. I was frightened.

By the time we got to Charing Cross he was back to his normal chirpy self. I explained this to the consultant, who decided to admit him to hospital straight away, for my sake and for observing Philip. He told me that they had booked an operation for 4 June but it was possible that they would bring this forward.

The following day Philip was fitted with a twenty-four hour tape to monitor his heart; it was a small portable machine like a walkman, but it was heavy. He put up with it so well, trotting about with it on his back like a rucksack. He played happily for the rest of the day and got ready for bed with no problems. Sitting on my knee, he dozed off to sleep. He slept very well that night although he did have a sedative at sometime in the early hours. I woke the next morning at 6am after a reasonable night's sleep, feeling queasy. I had some breakfast then went for a walk to the paper shop.

On my return I woke Philip, gave him his medicine then his breakfast. He was still a bit drowsy but chatted away. He came off the monitor and we went for a walk round the shops. Sister asked us to be back on the ward for about 11am so he could have a bath and get ready for his operation. On our way back from the shops we called into the hospital shop and he chose a toy lorry for me to buy.

We returned to the ward and Philip played with his new lorry, then it was time to get ready for the operation. He knew he was having an operation, and that he would have tubes in his mouth and tummy. Philip had his bath and played with some toys. He really enjoyed playing with the water. When we put on his special nightie, he asked if he was a nurse now. I told him that as he didn't have a hat he must be a doctor. I wrapped him up in a blanket then held him. Even then I felt that this may be the last time that I would cuddle him. I was glad we'd been for a walk and played in the bath, but the feeling that Philip would soon be gone got stronger.

Don and our friend Kathy came about 11.30am while I was cuddling Philip and I was crying. I didn't want to let go, yet in my heart I felt it was inevitable. The nurse came round and gave him his premed. Both Don and I nursed him and cuddled him. He dozed off to sleep. Just before he went to the operating theatre he woke and asked for a drink. Nurse Caroline came and took him to the theatre. He was crying but was very sleepy.

Don, Kathy and I went for something to eat then for a walk. Don and I returned to the hospital, then Don left to collect Rebecca, our daughter.

It was shortly after Don had left that Mary, the Liaison Officer, told me that Philip was having

problems. I asked to go to the chapel. I sobbed my
heart out; the noise echoed around the tall Victorian
chapel. Then I prayed that God would restart Philip's
heart, I prayed we wouldn't lose him. Then I said, if
not, let him go in peace. Praying the Lord's Prayer,
I said "Your will be done." My tears stopped and I
felt warm and tingly inside. I also felt God say to
me, "I have answered your prayer." As I felt calm
and composed I returned to the ward.

Shortly afterwards Mary and the surgeon came
to tell me that Philip had died on the operating
table. They had tried to start his heart for nearly two
hours. The surgeons had carried out the operation
which involved cutting away some of the heart
muscle. The remaining muscle was too thick to
restart pumping on its own so they were unable to
switch off the heart-lung machine. I felt devastated,
yet I knew Philip was all right.

They took me to see him a little later. I was
frightened, but I needn't have been. He was lying
with his hands on his chest, very still but with a look
of peace. He looked beautiful. I will treasure that
picture always. He looked like an angel. I stroked
his face and hands and played with his hair. I told
him that I'd look after his teddy, and that he'd never
be sick or poorly again. Then I kissed him and said,
"Good night, God bless." I thank God for those
precious three years and for all who looked after
and cared for Philip in those last days and hours.

The days and weeks following Philip's death
were hard for Hazel and me. Our hearts broke as

we grasped his ghost. Some thought we would lose our faith because of these losses. Yet in many ways, my faith was strengthened by what had happened. Jesus said, "He who loves father or mother more than me is not worthy of me. And he who loves son or daughter more than me is not worthy of me." (Matthew 10:37). The key to life is putting Jesus first, in all things. This is the only way to peace. What had happened was not God's doing. Jesus said, "The thief does not come except to steal, and to kill, and to destroy. I have come that they may have life, and that they may have it more abundantly." (John 10:10). Satan's plan for everyone is to steal, kill and destroy. The plan of Jesus is life in abundance. Clearly the hallmark of this experience was 'steal, kill and destroy'. It was part of the ongoing warfare to destroy God's people and eliminate leadership in the church. Man is a spiritual being as well as a physical one. We live in two worlds and trace on the walls of our cave the wonders and the nightmares of our existence.

I had sometimes prayed to be like Jesus. I'd forgotten that Isaiah called him, "a man of sorrows and acquainted with grief". I finished training for the ministry a few weeks later, wounded and well acquainted with grief.

Chapter 7

The archbishop and the burglar

The organ thundered through Southwark cathedral, standing by London Bridge, as the capacity congregation sang out 'Christ is made the sure foundation...' I took my place in the long procession with Church Army evangelists about to be commissioned. Various clergy and cathedral staff followed behind us, the Chief Secretary, Michael Rees, with the college Principal and the Archbishop of Canterbury, Robert Runcie, brought up the rear. Commissioning day had arrived at last. It was the end of three years of training and yet only the beginning of full-time ministry.

My personal grief and loss had been the backdrop to a busy three years of training – daily lectures on theology, Biblical studies, church history and evangelism. I had been on many placements during training. I had spent a month working with the chaplaincy at Wandsworth Prison. Shadowing Captain David Kearns and other chaplains, I gained a first-hand view of prison chaplaincy. I spent some time on a wing with paedophiles. Some were in denial. One tried to intimidate me when I was shut in his cell. I led an outreach service where several men gave their life to Christ and also saw individuals come to Jesus as we spoke to them privately in their cells. Underlying the success of the chaplaincy was daily devotional prayer as a team.

I had the privilege of going with David to a lunch at his church, held in the home of Norman Warren, author of 'Journey into Life', which had such an impact on my life years before.

We did Tuesday afternoon placements on 'Open Air' meetings. Our group went down to New Cross, near Blackheath. The other teams had all the musicians so it was hard to sing. We stood opposite a betting shop in our best uniforms, watched with interest by a group of Rastafarians. As our guitarist could only play Sunday School tunes, we began to sing these twee little children's songs much to the amusement of the Rastas. A group of about fifty Millwall football supporters came round the corner, each carrying a crate of beer, consuming it as they went. They were all singing football chants on the way to the match. At this opportune moment our leader, Captain Roy Demery, poked me in the back and said, "Right, you give a testimony." I really wanted the ground to swallow me up. Cultures were clashing and I felt we, dressed in our victorian uniforms, definitely seemed the least relevant. It was a make or break situation.

I stepped forward and boldly began to tell how Jesus Christ had changed my life. As I began the first few words, a holy boldness came upon me. I was now surrounded by the Millwall supporters who continued to chant and drink. One of them, a tattooed skinhead holding a crate of beer, stopped right in front of me and looked me in the eye. He listened for a moment and then said, "You really believe that, don't you?"

"Yes, I do." I replied.

He walked off, chanting his slogans. Something happened to me that day that broke through my shyness. Once you have stood your ground and told of God's goodness to a bunch of yelling football yobs, you really can tell anybody in any situation!

I also spent several weeks at Crowhurst, a community of healing near Hastings. I took services and preached at several services a day and lived as part of the community. I took part in a college mission to several parishes in Exeter and saw what can be achieved with a strong evangelistic team as we reached out onto a council estate. I had also done several parish placements in London and my final placement at St Luke's Benchill, in Manchester, where we moved after college.

The service at Southwark cathedral progressed and we were all duly commissioned to our various posts. After a big reception, back at the college, we all prepared for our respective moves.

Hazel and I arrived in Manchester to the problem housing estate of Benchill, Wythenshawe. Originally, a 'garden city' – a show-piece of modern social engineering. "Give people gardens and space and all will be well." And all had been well for the original 1930s tenants who had left the slums of Manchester's city centre. But after years of the policy of moving all the 'problem families' out to Wythenshawe, all was not well. Crime and vandalism had reached overwhelming levels. It wasn't long before I realised we were virtually under siege every night from local vandals. One night when I had calmly reasoned with them, they came and smashed our car windows. The building we lived in was formerly the old Sunday School rooms at the back of the church. It had unwisely been built on the water-table and with a flat roof. When it rained, as it often does in Manchester, not only did the roof leak but water came up through the floor soaking the carpets. I was often on the roof in storms, fighting battles with leaks using underwater sealant designed for oil rigs.

Benchill had a large aged population, a consequence of which was a high volume of funerals. Oliver Foreshaw, the vicar, took most of them but inevitably I also took hundreds during our time there. The very thing I feared, being seen as a pseudo-curate, had come upon me.

I gained some relief from occasional visits to Mansfield, where Kerry Dixon had been posted. It was always good to meet and share the joys and sorrows of ministry. I also went to preach at St John's Mansfield a few times at the invitation of Kerry's vicar, Ken Shill. On one of these visits Kerry was recruiting people to join him on Church Army's Norfolk Broads holiday mission. I loved boats and agreed to join him. Kerry had been given leadership of the mission after being on placement on the Broads Mission during college days. I happily joined the team as we visited pubs along the Broads and shared our faith. We started with a puppet show and had a professional singer booked as entertainment in the beer gardens, as the backdrop to one-to-one conversations. We distributed lots of literature and generally found people willing to talk about spiritual matters and some ready to receive Jesus personally. In one place, a member of the team sat with the pub chef who was watching the puppet show. He showed him a prayer of commitment in the book 'Journey into Life' and said, "Is there any reason why you can't pray that prayer right now?" To his amazement, the chef said, "I would like to pray that prayer. I have heard the gospel many times and have never responded. Recently I have felt I should do something about it." He received Jesus there and then.

In the first week we had the singer Paul Poulton and his wife Lorraine with us. In the second week we had the talents of David Lyle Morris from New Zealand. These were happy days for me, on boats in the summer sunshine, talking of Jesus and meeting new teams – though it was always hard to leave Hazel and Rebecca behind yet again.

During the two years we were at Benchill, I was constantly searching for something. It was as though all my past had been stolen. My parents, my childhood home, our son and my place in my home district and church – all had been lost. On days off I sometimes visited the places of my childhood but many were gone. Gone was the station at Clayton

Bridge where we used to watch the trains steam by. Oh, the endless searching for yesterday...

Then one day, it's hard to say when exactly, I realised that God had healed my broken heart. He had taken the grief away. It was not time that had healed, as some suppose, no. There was a definite work of God. A new heart beat inside me, one that looked to the future with hope and did not always dwell on the past. Frustrated with the work and accommodation, we began to talk of moving to a new place and starting again.

Just after Christmas, we had a call from Felixstowe to say that little Kylie, who had lain in the next bed to our son, Philip, in hospital, had died in her mother's arms of the same illness. We travelled to be with her family at the funeral on New Year's Eve. As we travelled through Suffolk we stopped at a petrol station. When we pulled out from there, to continue our journey, I looked across the fields to the market town coming up on the horizon and pointed. "This would be a nice place to live," I said, pointing to houses across a field.

"Yes, it would," said Hazel. (Six months later, this is where we lived!)

We continued to Kylie's funeral in Ipswich and then met with the family in Felixstowe. We set off back to Manchester. As we arrived in Manchester, midnight was approaching and we went to Hazel's parents to collect Rebecca and see in the new year with them. We arrived home at about one o'clock to find that we had been burgled. They didn't take much – just the TV and video recorder. These were currency in the drug culture that surrounded us. The feeling of being invaded when we had no emotional reserves was too much for us to bear. It seemed like the last straw.

Hazel was now pregnant and we just felt this was not the best place to bring up children. A few days later I phoned Church Army to impress upon them the urgency of our need to move. They said there was nothing available but when I pressed the matter, they said there may be something in East Anglia. I had no idea where East Anglia was but, as the words were spoken, peace came upon me. I knew we would be going there sometime.

Heather was born that Easter – a new life came to our home and we had the usual joys and trials of a newborn baby. Heather grew and became a very active child. One can never replace a child who has died, but there was an element of healing in Heather's arrival. Life began to seem more normal. Her arrival seemed to draw a line under the mourning and usher in a new season of hope.

After a series of interviews, we received notification that I had been accepted as the Parish Evangelist for St Peter's Stowmarket in Suffolk replacing the much-loved curate, John Ross. We had several farewells including a surprise farewell dinner with my Church Army colleagues. Ian Ferguson tricked us into going for dinner with him, only for us to be greeted by members of the Church Army Area Staff Meeting, where I had been secretary for eighteen months. It was a very unexpected but encouraging evening with some very special people.

In many ways my time at Benchill felt like failure. Our personal grief, my inexperience in ministry and the constant battle with local vandals had left me little energy to be pioneering at St Luke's, which is what was needed. I'd conducted hundreds of funerals during this time, which wasn't entirely helpful. They kept me surrounded by grief. We were there only two years but it felt much longer. As we followed the removal van out of the church drive, and began our long journey south, I was glad this dark chapter was over and I set my face towards Suffolk without a backward glance.

Chapter 8

The insurance man, the Freemason and the rope cutter

In 1989 we arrived in Stowmarket, in sleepy Suffolk. The contrast with where we had come from could not have been sharper. Instead of a leaky, damp home, we were provided with a nearly new four bedroomed house on the edge of town overlooking the fields. There was so little crime we sometimes didn't even bother to lock the doors at night. There was a lot less rain than in Manchester and things were done a lot slower. Some people have even referred to the town as Slow-market. For the first six months it felt like being on holiday from the grinding crime-ridden estates of Benchill.

The welcome at St Peter's was overwhelming. To this day, I feel I owe a lot to the kindness and encouragement of the congregation at St Peter's. As I stood up to preach on the first Sunday there was spontaneous applause. I'm still not sure why. My predecessor, John Ross, was a man's man and had been very successful in reaching and converting many men in the parish. He had also left a group of people keen to see evangelism take place. He had set up a monthly evangelistic service called 'Open Door' one Sunday evening a month. The worship band was in the ascendant and the robed choir was in decline. I tried to keep the idea of outreach on the agenda but many things, in reality, became mere 'indrag'. We were good at putting on events but not so good at bringing people to them.

In some ways, I found myself in an awkward place for an evangelist – all my relationships were with Christians. Being a newcomer to the area, I had no non-church relationships. I decided to make some inroads by engaging in a few non-church activities. I had always wanted to play a musical instrument. I improvised on the piano occasionally but had never had any training. I found a man in town who taught saxophone and enrolled in a few lessons. Eventually I bought an alto-sax and practised at home, much to Hazel's amusement and irritation. Bruce, my instructor, used to arrange a jazz evening at the 'Pine Mines', a bar in the centre of town. For most of the evening, people who could really play performed. For the last two or three songs, anyone with a sax – mainly Bruce's students – could join the band and perform. As there wasn't always time to tune up, the dozen or so saxophones sometimes made a racket rather than music but it was fun.

The bishops of the Anglican church had made a pronouncement that the closing decade of the millennium should be a 'decade of evangelism'. They said churches should move away from a pastoral model of church and from maintenance to mission. It did put evangelism on the map but it was really up to individuals to make it happen and bring about the needed change.

My own response was to try and make as much of the church activity as possible evangelistic, or at least make it accessible to non-believers. I didn't really have a plan but tried to adapt and use what was going on to reach out with good news.

When summer came, we entered a church float in the carnival and even won a prize! We put the music group on the back of a lorry and pumped out the best of Graham Kendrick's songs, which were the latest thing in worship at the time.

One year, we even had a stand on the fairground when Kerry Dixon brought across the Church Army stage show lorry. Kerry performed various acts of escapology and I presented the show. I was also chained up and put in a sack with a noose round my neck and escaped just in the nick of time. Kerry disappeared from a coffin and magically appeared in the crowd. We then shared the story of how Jesus came to set us free from death.

I took on the parish magazine and tried to make the cover story evangelistic and thought-provoking. A man who had recently become a Christian and joined the church was a graphic designer. His name was Peter Goodsell and he was very helpful to me in redesigning the magazine and other church leaflets for outsiders. Peter also played the sax and was part of the group who performed at the Pine Mines. He became a great personal friend and we shared many interests.

An article I wrote against Freemasonry was very provocative to some and I was reported to the bishop.

A Mason left the church. It rippled through the town where some were trying to mix Freemasonry with Christianity which, to this day, I find an insult to Christ.

A group of men approached me asking for more Bible teaching and more opportunities for evangelism. Evenings were always busy and they all had full-time jobs, so time was a problem. One of the men, Andy, and I went for lunch one day and discussed the matter. As we talked I had an idea. Why don't we go to the pub once a week for a Bible study? We can learn together there. If we get talking to the regulars, then we will be doing evangelism as well. So that is what happened. A group of about six of us met every week in a local pub. We took our Bibles and some evangelistic literature. We could relax and talk about the things of God. It proved a stroke of genius.

One man had been telling his insurance man about the love of God and invited him to church.

"Never!" he said. "You'll never get me inside a church!"

With great ease he was able to say, "Well how about the pub? Do you have any problem going there?"

"No," said the insurance man.

He came the following night to the pub meeting and fired all his questions, doubts and fears at us. At the end of the night I gave him a John's gospel and a copy of 'Journey into Life'. The following Sunday he was in church. He had gone home, read the booklet and prayed a prayer asking Jesus into his life. As he did he had a very powerful encounter with Jesus. His life changed and he came to church.

Some nights there were very few people in the pub so we had a look at some scriptures together. The evangelist in me noticed the landlady listening intently. When one of the men tried to talk to her she didn't want to know. As we left, I purposely left one of our booklets on the table.

The following week as we sat down, the landlady marched up to us straight away. "Do you have any more of those booklets you left last week?" she said. "I read it after you went and said that prayer at the end. I showed it to my mother-in-law. She read it and prayed the prayer. She showed it to all the old people that live in her flats. They all prayed the prayer and all asked if they could have a copy of the book."

Amazed at how simple this encounter had been, I gave her a dozen or so booklets. She began attending a church in Ipswich, to where she later moved to take on a new pub.

On another occasion, just before closing time, a group of four of us met two ladies. One of them was quite belligerent and making anti-Christian remarks. As we moved to leave, she told us she had gone out that night to commit suicide and only the chance meeting of her friend stopped her and had brought her to the pub. As I listened, I noticed that there was no one else in the bar – even the barman was in the other bar collecting glasses. I offered to pray with her there and then. She accepted and the four of us laid hands on her right there in the pub. She found a new peace she had never encountered before.

Now doesn't that sound like a story from the gospels, with Jesus ministering to people, not always in the temple, but right where they are – at weddings, at dinners, on the road, in the pub? Truly the fields are white for harvest.

The following year, I invited my good friend Ian Ferguson down for a weekend of mission and we held one of the meetings in that same pub. Just before he came, the Strangeways riots happened and the prison was on every TV news bulletin. By the time Ian arrived he had a ready audience in the pub. We laid on some sandwiches and extended the bar opening into the afternoon. The church folk sat at one end of the bar and the regulars at the other. Ian and I sat in the middle. I introduced him and handed him the microphone. When he finished speaking, the regulars gathered round him and wanted to know more. However, the leap from the pub meeting to middle-class church service was too far for them. I began to become convinced that a new sort of church may be required to disciple people who were clearly interested in Jesus but had no interest in traditional church services. The culture and world-view of each group was too far apart.

It was a Saturday morning when a letter arrived from Church Army asking me to become the leader of the Norfolk Broads Summer Mission. It was a big shock. Kerry Dixon had always led that mission and I had always been a key partner in that arrangement. I always saw myself as someone who had input into other people's projects but never as a leader. I phoned Kerry and he told me he had been invited to lead the Blackpool mission and I had been the obvious person to take over leadership of the Norfolk Broads Mission. As ever, Kerry talked me through the process and it began to feel OK. By nature, I'm an implementer. My first thought about any project or task is how we get from A to B and beyond. The structure was already there and all I needed to do was to follow the rough plan.

February is a bleak time on the Norfolk Broads. The area relies heavily on the tourist trade and holidaymakers hiring boats. In winter, a peaceful silence hangs over the Broads, as though the area rests from the frenetic activity of the summer. This was the time of year when preparations began for the summer mission. I visited the twenty-odd pubs along the various river banks and got the permission of each landlord to come in the summer with a professional singer, a puppet show and a team of helpers. I had mapped out the planned summer route we would take – Church Army financed a holiday cruiser for the team and we visited one or two pubs and riverbanks each day with music, puppets and a chance to chat. It seemed like a long way to go in the winter, just for a brief chat with each landlord but it really smoothed the way and avoided disappointment in the summer.

For five years, I led the summer mission on the Norfolk Broads. I took a team of 8 to 10 people, drawn from various churches and connections, who were keen on evangelism. We would always employ a professional singer as this was the key to getting the ground in the beer gardens or sometimes even inside pubs. Some years we had Paul Poulton and his wife Lorraine. The great thing about Paul and Lorraine was that, in addition to Paul being a very competent musician and entertainer, Lorraine was a keen evangelist as well.

Other years, my good friend David Lyle Morris provided the music and was a valuable member of the team. David is from New Zealand and would sometimes dress up as a Mowori warrior and burst into the team's bedrooms in the middle of the night, letting out an ear-piercing war cry. David later went to work for Graham Kendrick for a few years, before returning to his homeland of New Zealand where he now lives with his wife and children.

Leading the Broads mission for those years was a real privilege, as I love steering large boats, mooring up right in the middle of all the Broadland wildlife, and seeing people come to know Jesus or take a step closer.

One night we had obviously upset someone as, under cover of darkness, they cut our mooring ropes. As we slept, our cruiser drifted downstream as the tide went out towards Great Yarmouth. It could have been very dangerous, even fatal. When we woke in the morning, Paul Poulton informed us that the pub that had been outside his bedroom window last night was now missing! As we emerged outside we were completely lost. A heavy mist had descended during the night and we were surrounded by thick fog. The boat had come to rest on a bank of reeds. Like Moses' basket, we had come to rest in the bulrushes and were quite safe. We took a smaller boat up-river to establish where we were. When we returned to our moorings, there was the other end of the rope clearly cut though on purpose. A small price to pay for what we were doing.

The summer missions were a great training ground for people in the parish to try more intense mission. It also helped keep me focussed on the main thing. The summer missions to the Broads were for two weeks a year. On the middle Sunday, members of St Peter's Stowmarket would usually come up from Suffolk and share in leading an open-air service. It was always good to see Hazel and the girls at this halfway point in the mission too. I think I can safely say that the year which will always stand out in people's memory is the year that, as the St Peter's gang arrived at Ranworth Staithe, they watched me slip, as I climbed from the dinghy to the main boat, and disappear under the waters of the Broad with a splosh, only to surface a moment later looking green and decidedly damp. Great summers those.

Chapter 9

I give up!

It was some time in 1992. Ministry just seemed like one compromise after another and one tradition and piece of history blocking another avenue for evangelism. It seemed like that. In reality, my own negative attitude and my wonderful ability to blame others aggravated difficult situations. Being in the position of psuedo-curate really wasn't helping. I hadn't signed up for this.

The accumulation of being in the wrong position and seeing few of the great promises that had been spoken over me coming to pass, brought me to the end of myself. I made a decision in my heart that I would see things through to the end of next year, 1993, and then I would quit the ministry. I'd had enough and it wasn't working. I settled it and, in my mind, I laid the ministry down.

It was about this time that I got a call to say one of my younger brothers was seriously ill. I eventually spoke to him on the phone. He'd been in hospital with suspected diabetes and become frustrated with waiting for a proper diagnosis. Eventually he'd checked himself out of the hospital. As a result he had suffered massive nerve damage which resulted in crippling shooting pains through his arms several times a day. He'd also been passing out while his house-mate was at work and woke up on the floor. I travelled up to Manchester and stayed with him for a couple of days to try and get a measure of the situation. Things seemed very serious.

I suggested that he come and stay with us in Suffolk for a few days. It was awful seeing him in such agony. His symptoms were far from typical and this was making it difficult for the doctors to find the right medication.

During one of his stays with us, he ran out of steroids which he was taking to combat the effect of nerve damage. It was a Bank Holiday and it was difficult to get a prescription when his doctor was back in Manchester. During a walk in town he collapsed. I drove him home but things just got worse. I called an ambulance and he was rushed to hospital. Eventually, after waiting hours, his medication was replaced and he became stable.

As a result of this and the trips back and forward to Manchester, I suggested he should come and live with us for a while. His eyesight had been badly affected and we spent hours in the hospital, on countless trips, while he had laser treatment to save his sight. He lived with us for a whole year as he slowly recovered.

As usual, that December, I joined four hundred other evangelists at Swanwick in Derbyshire for the Evangelists' conference. The speaker that year was Dr R. T. Kendal from Westminster Chapel in London. He was teaching on the life of King David. One of his messages was entitled, 'The Anointing without the Crown'. He told of David's life between being anointed as king and taking up the crown. How David's character was tested and honed by God. It wasn't enough to have the anointing but the character also had to be formed. His anointing would get him through the door but good character would keep him there.

As Dr Kendall preached, I felt God saying, "You have the anointing but you don't yet have the crown. Be patient. It will come." With the benefit of hindsight, it is all so much clearer now. Life is best understood backwards but it has to be lived forwards. It is clear to me now that character may be manifested in great moments but it is formed in small ones. I had a lot to learn. I also had no idea what was about to happen.

I returned from Swanwick ready to continue in ministry. I had still laid the ministry down but was ready to do that which God gave back. It did release me from striving to make things happen. I am very grateful to R. T. Kendall for that message and the way God used it to keep me in the ministry. Billy Graham said that most evangelists give up after ten years. I almost became one of them.

Chapter 10

The miraculous pork pie and the custard army

"Gentlemen, I have seen a vision of one thousand men, walking down the 'spine of England' – the Pennine Way, re-enacting the Acts of the Apostles – going from town to town and village to village, sharing the good news of Christ in pubs, in schools, on the streets and from house to house."

The almost Churchillian tones of Anglican evangelist Daniel Cozens, on a tape, stirred my heart, as Kerry Dixon and I headed off to another Norfolk Broads Mission. Daniel was sharing his vision to raise up an army of evangelists – one thousand men to be precise – to walk the Pennine Way, to live simply and share their faith wherever they went. Teams of ten men would be overseen by leaders who in turn would be overseen by centurions. A limit of two pounds a day would be imposed to teach men to live simply and trust God day by day. What a challenge!

It sounded a tall order and Daniel faced much opposition and some ridicule as he initially struggled to get the numbers. But a few months later, I found myself climbing out of a minibus in the Pennines and being moved by the sight of hundreds of men in green sweatshirts, with the mission logo emblazoned on their chest – 'How beautiful on the mountains are the feet of him who brings good news' – milling

about and ready for two or three weeks of action
and adventure for the Kingdom of God.

The locals dubbed it 'the invasion of the green
men'. Our team arrived on the hills and set off for a
twelve-mile walk, with heavy rucksacks, to Hawes,
the village where the James Herriot TV series,
about a vet, had been filmed. We were billeted in a
farmhouse with a shepherd and his family. For three
days, we visited homes, pubs and schools telling the
good news of Jesus. We went from door to door and
met a lady who had heard we were coming. After
chatting to her for a few minutes on her doorstep,
she took a booklet from us and said 'goodbye'.
That night she came to a meeting in a restaurant and
told how she had read the booklet, knelt down and
prayed a prayer asking Jesus to come into her life.
There were countless such stories on this mission.
The fields are indeed white for harvest.

Later in the mission, we walked to Hebden
Bridge, where no arrangements had been made
except that the team of ten men could sleep on a
church hall floor. It was called 'Open Fields' and we
were to just pray and see what God would do. By this
time all our money was gone. The men had walked
twelve miles in bad weather and gone to bed with
very little food. There was nothing for the next day.
When daybreak came and we all woke, we prayed
that God would send some breakfast. There was a
real anointing on the prayer time as we worshipped
together in that church hall. As we prayed, Kerry
felt moved to go and stand on the street corner and

continue to pray. The rest of us continued in prayer in the hall. Never before had the words, "Give us today our daily bread," had such meaning. As Kerry stood on the corner, a local pastor came by walking his dog.

"What are you standing there for?" the pastor asked Kerry.

"I am just standing here praying for bread for the team's breakfast," he replied.

"Well, come with me," said the pastor. "I have a freezer full of bread!"

Kerry returned to the hall with a big smile and an even bigger carrier bag full of bread. In the church kitchen we found some butter, jam and coffee, so it was hot toast and coffee all round. That was breakfast sorted out but the rest of the day was ahead of us and we had no idea if we would eat again that day.

However, as instructed, we went out and looked for some spontaneous opportunity to share the good news. There was no obvious opening, so some of the men suggested we went to the park to sing and preach in the open air and see what happened. It felt like it would have a high cringe factor to me but in the absence of any better ideas, that's what we did.

As you would expect, most people gave these strange men in green sweaters a wide berth, perhaps supposing we were from some cult. That was, all apart from a young lady and an old man. The lady sat right on the bench where one of the men stood preaching. As we chatted she told us why she was there.

"I became a Christian last week," she began. "But a strange thing has just happened. I was in the bakers and I found myself buying this large pork pie. The thing is, I don't like pork pie. My children don't like it and nor does my husband. But I felt I really needed to buy it. So I have come into the park to ask God what is happening and what I should do with it."

We told her our story and what the mission was about and how we had no food or money.

"Well, that's it!" she said. "God has sent me to buy it for you!"

It was was a terrific pie!

Meanwhile one of the men was talking with the old man, who felt lost in the world and readily received Jesus into his heart.

As we met the rest of the men at the end of the second week change-over briefing, there really were hundreds of similar stories of God's provision and his opening doors into people's lives. It was an exhausting week but what an experience. Daniel has since gone on to mobilise thousands of men from churches all over the country and has led several 'Walk Missions' across the nation. I led another team on 'Walk Kent' some years later.

It was a windy and wet night, as Kerry Dixon and I walked through Westminster in London. The light

from the shop windows reflected in the wet roads
as the endless traffic passed by. We had been at the
Church Army Area Secretaries' Christmas dinner,
in London Victoria, meeting with the Chairman
of the Board, and decided to have a walk before
turning in for the night at our accommodation. We
walked through the damp streets and talked of our
vision to see revival in Britain. How we hoped to
see the things we had read of in the lives of people
like John Wesley, George Whitefield and the stories
of Rees Howells and the Welsh revival. As Big Ben
struck eleven, we found ourselves at the Houses of
Parliament. The presence of God seemed so close.
We prayed for our nation to see revival in our day.
We prayed that there would be a sea change in the
country and the nation would turn back to God.
I really felt God confirm to us that we would see
revival in our day and that he could still touch the
nation and bring thousands back to himself. All
around us the London traffic splashed through the
wet streets but, in the shadows of the parliament
building, there was a holy moment for two young
men.

Back in Stowmarket, pressure was growing for
me to lead a town-wide mission. I had been on
countless badly organised missions (as well as a few
really good ones), so I was keen that, if I organised
a mission for St Peter's, it should avoid some of
the pitfalls I had seen and be properly financed. In
those days, as now, I was in the habit of walking
around the fields which surround Stowmarket, for

about an hour most mornings, to pray, think and meditate before the day started. On one particular morning, I woke very early as the sun was rising. I got up and went out early into the deserted fields. I was praying about the possible mission and seeking God's leading.

As I reached the bottom corner of the farmer's field, I got an urge to stop and turn round. As I did, I saw a large red sun coming up from behind a tree. As I looked at the sun through the tree, the tree seemed to be on fire but not consumed – just like the burning bush of Moses. I stood for some time looking at the picture before me and had an encounter with God. It was as though the vision for the mission had been imparted in that experience. I got back home and began writing down what I saw as the vision for the mission called RSVP '93.

It was to be based around a large tent on the Recreation Ground. Yet it would also reach into schools, pubs and other places across the town. There would be mission beer mats in pubs, like those used by Daniel Cozens in the Walk Missions. Teams would go to the pubs each night while the meetings were on in the tent. There would be after-school clubs and the mission would last ten days. Kerry Dixon and my friend Ken Ashby would be the preachers, while I would lead the meetings.

I presented the plan to the Church Council with a budget of £6,000 over two years. Amazingly it was all accepted. In reality, the final budget doubled to nearer £12,000. The mission touched the town and brought the church together like never before. I can't think of another event in Stowmarket when the strict Baptists and the Roman Catholics attended the same meeting. More importantly, some significant people took a step of faith during that mission and committed their life to Christ.

There were lots of lessons learned during the mission. There were also a few disasters along the way. I had been impressed on the Walk Missions by the impact of the team all wearing a mission sweater. I wanted to bring about the same effect in Stowmarket. I wondered about the colour we should choose. The tent we ordered was shown in the catalogue to be predominantly yellow and white. In an attempt to link the team with the yellow tent on the recreation ground, I ordered hundreds of yellow sweaters with the mission logo on.

What I failed to realise was, yellow does not suit a lot of people and they don't want to wear it. The yellow sweaters nearly caused mass mutiny, with a lot of people getting hot under the collar. Added to that, when the tent was finally erected, it was white – the yellow one had been replaced! In the end people were gracious and all wore the yellow sweaters. Word came back that the town had dubbed us 'The Custard Army'. One of my enduring memories of that mission was Richard Stretch and Phil Kinder in their yellow sweaters cycling round the town on Richard's bright yellow tandem – Richard steering and Phil announcing the mission events with a hand-held megaphone. It certainly put the mission on the town agenda.

During this mission, Kerry had asked me to go with him on a three-week mission to the Philippines. I really didn't want to go. I had never travelled abroad and was very fussy about food. I prayed that I would not have to go. Yet, deep within, I knew that this could be the beginning of the fulfilment of the vision I had in the Lake District as a young man – that I would preach in other nations. I was staring my greatest fears in the face and I didn't want to go. I felt God was a little amused that East Anglia was the most dangerous place I was willing to go!

On the last night of the mission, I was standing at the entrance of the tent saying goodbye to people when my friend Miriam Smith approached me. Miriam was in her seventies and prayed for me every day. She was a short, blunt Yorkshire lass who seldom minced her words.

"I was praying for you yesterday," she said. "God gave me a message for you. He told me to tell you to 'Go into all the world and preach the gospel!'"

The words cut into me like a sword. As Miriam spoke those words, Kerry's invitation to the Philippines now became God's express command to go. I recognised his voice in my heart. The tent mission had crowned my five years at Stowmarket and one sensed the page was turning and a new chapter was beginning. I needed to raise £1,200 for the trip and I really couldn't see where that was going to come from. But I agreed that if God provided, I would go to the Philippines for three weeks with Kerry. It was now September and the trip was planned for December that year.

Shortly after the Stowmarket mission, my brother found a flat and moved to live independently. Soon he found a job locally and decided to stay in Suffolk. The mission, and our family situation during that time, had really stretched me to the limit. I was out of my depth on many fronts. The water, however, was about to get much deeper.

Chapter 11

Appointment in Asia

Twenty-one hours and three flights after leaving the December chill in England, Kerry Dixon and I, along with our friend Wendy Diaper, stepped off a high-tech jumbo jet into the sweltering humidity and Third-World poverty of the Philippines. In Manila international airport everything seemed thirty years out of date, mainly because it was.

Immigration and customs officials shouted things at me in a language I couldn't understand. As we emerged into the foyer, we ran the gauntlet of hundreds of taxi drivers wanting our custom. Out of this chaos we emerged to find a minibus which took us to the domestic airport.

We raced through the dark, sweltering night in what seemed like a banger race – most of the cars looked like they had come straight from the scrapyard. Many of them drove through the night without lights. What one noticed immediately was the ubiquitous jeepney.

These American troop carriers, left behind when the Americans left the islands, had been decorated in garish Filipino style and became the main mode of transportation. Decorated with slogans and chrome, and with their distinctive 'beep-beep', they raced down every road like a flock of excited roadrunners. At the domestic airport we were locked out for hours and had to sleep on the pavement with everyone else until it opened. It was 10.30pm and our flight was not until 4am.

The air was filled with the stench of sewage mixed with the sweet and spicy smells from the pavement stalls, cooking nuts and other snacks. All this blended with the general air pollution to produce an atmosphere that makes everyone gag.

As we sat on the floor in the foyer outside the airport, a few cleaners emerged and rearranged the dirt on the foyer floor and windows. A lone urchin squatted in the shadows against the wall begging. He looked about seven years old. A couple of small lizards stood guard by a flickering light fitting, catching mosquitoes attracted to its light. A large cockroach passed by and disappeared into the shadows. Suddenly, I felt a long way from home.

As we came in to land at Iloilo City airport at 5.30am, I saw the shanty houses of the poor built right up to the side of the runway. The airport is a single runway with a small office block at one end. I felt exhausted and was having second thoughts about coming but that was about to change. Although it was so early, a group of church members stood in the airport waiting for our arrival. As they saw us, they unfurled a welcome banner, put garlands of flowers around our necks and broke into a song of welcome. Their smiles lit up our hearts. They were so thankful we had come.

The hazy morning sun was climbing through the

humid air into the sky. We clambered into a jeep and shared stories and laughter, relieved our long journey was nearly completed. We drove for miles to a suburb of Iloilo, past mile after mile of bamboo shacks – the small unofficial villages of the poor known as 'barangays'. Pastor Ed Fernadez, our host, lived in one of these barangays. His home was currently under threat as the government had sold the land to a multinational company who were planning to bulldoze the homes off their land to make way for a large factory unit.

We arrived at Ed's house – a small bamboo and plywood house of about five rooms. As we unloaded our bags from the jeep, I had a strange encounter. Through the humid haze of the early morning, coming across the fields of banana and palm trees, the presence of God swept over me with great power. "I will be with you always, even to the ends of the earth." I heard the voice of God. I felt overwhelmed by his love. For me, geographically and emotionally, this was indeed the ends of the earth. It would be difficult to get any further away from home.

I regained my composure and joined the others in the house at a simple breakfast of eggs and bananas which Dottie, Ed's wife, had prepared. Wendy was staying in the city, so Kerry and I were shown to our room here at Ed's.

It was a typical shanty house room with a gap between the top of the wall and the corrugated iron roof, to keep the tropical air moving. It was a dimly lit humid cell and, in the evenings, a rendezvous for every cockroach, gecko and insect in the city. This would be my home for the next two weeks.

We were taken on a tour of Iloilo City and to the church building, which was on the third floor of an office building in the city centre. It was here that the church linked with various overseas groups to run a successful child sponsorship project.

As we toured the city we discovered a branch of Dunkin' Doughnuts – a small oasis of western civilisation. I made a daily pilgrimage here throughout my time in Iloilo, not only because the food was more familiar but it was one of the few places in the city that had air-conditioning. It was a sanctuary in the sweltering, unremitting heat of the Philippines.

In the evening, we returned to Ed's house. A supper of chicken heads and legs had been prepared. Mercifully the legs were for us. After coffee and a chat with Ed we turned in for bed at about nine o'clock. I tucked my mosquito net into my mattress and lay down for the night. 1 was emotionally swamped. I had to suppress all kinds of emotions – fear at the number and size of insects, repulsion at the lack of hygiene and being presented with things like pigs' intestines to eat, deep sorrow at seeing so many lovely people stuck in terrible poverty and feeling very homesick already.

As I settled down to sleep I heard the gecko – a lizard about two feet long that feeds on cockroaches.

It is seldom seen but in the darkness will come into the house looking for insects. Its name comes from the loud cuckoo-like noise it makes – 'gecko.' As it is only heard and not seen, this creature became a terrible legendary enemy to me. I began to imagine a lizard the size of a labrador wandering into the room. I also began to realise why Filipinos are so superstitious. With so many strange noises at night it was easy to see how one might imagine each noise as a goblin, witch or evil spirit.

After a hot and restless night we woke in the early hours of Friday to the sound of torrential rain. There was a tornado off the coast and the heavy rain was threatening floods. Emotionally I felt a little better after some sleep but it was hard not being able to phone home. I hoped Hazel and the girls were OK.

We couldn't go out in the rain, so we chatted to Ed and Dottie about things while we waited for it to stop. Kerry used the time to clarify things about the Helping Hands child sponsorship programme which had expanded rapidly to 200 children. Helping Hands was the church's child development project, sponsoring the education and medical care of children. Another 1,000 children awaited sponsorship which would radically change the future for their families and save them from continued poverty.

Eventually, we caught the jeepney for the five-mile trip into town. When we arrived at the church centre, a young man from the music group was assigned to take us round the shanty town. His name was Jijie. He became a very good friend to me.

We walked through the city, round a corner and suddenly turned down an alley. Instantly we seemed to have stepped into a scene from Jackie Pullinger's book, 'Chasing the Dragon'. Mile after mile of tin, wood and bamboo huts formed a maze of narrow passages. Sewage ran in streams along the way. Here and there lay dead rats. Barefoot and semi-naked children stared at us with large hungry eyes yet somehow still possessed that warm Filipino smile. Malnourished chickens and turkeys with one leg tied to the houses, flapped as we passed by. A dog, which might be some family's next meal, barked at us. Some of the houses looked substantially built. Others were little more than a few planks of wood leaning against a wall.

We passed by the fishing port gate and slipped down a passage to the sea front. I didn't think the smell could get worse but it did. There on the beach the dispossessed had built little shacks measuring less than six feet by eight feet. In these little bamboo huts, families of up to eight or nine people lived, suspended on bamboo stilts fifteen feet in the air, above the beach, which had now become a huge open sewer and refuse dump.

These bamboo shanty houses were reached by a maze of bamboo bridges. Built only to withstand the weight of a malnourished and shorter Filipino, these bridges began to give way under the weight of a taller and slightly overweight Westerner. The prospect of falling fifteen feet into the cesspit beach below filled me with dread. But my antics were causing a great deal of laughter to our now considerable entourage.

A fire had recently started in a barangay and spread rapidly through the timber village, making many families homeless. Thus they had come here to the beach to build their lives from scratch.

We met many children. Some were being sponsored by Helping Hands. Three children we found were left at home all day alone, aged six years, four years and eighteen months. Their mother had gone to Singapore for three years to begin a new life for them. After she had repaid her employers for the air fare and accommodation she would eventually be able to send for the rest of the family. Their father was a pastor but received no payment for his pastoring. He worked in a factory for two pounds a month in order to feed the children. Sometimes he returned home to find that one of the children had fallen from the house into the sewage below.

When I met the father later, he was deeply embarrassed that we had discovered his situation in this way. This was the plight of a family trying desperately to escape poverty so that their children didn't have to face the same predicament as they grew older. The alternative was to resign oneself to poverty as many had. Many of the people we met were born in these conditions. They would grow up and probably die prematurely in this place. We met many good, decent people living in such conditions.

Some homes were a little more established than others. They counted it such an honour to be visited by western Christians that they would often spend what little money they had that we might have a drink of Coke in their home. At this time, I had hundreds of pounds on me – the temptation was to insist that we paid for everything. But they requested the dignity to give us hospitality. It would have been most arrogant to refuse them. A very difficult lesson in humility indeed.

As darkness fell, Dottie took me back to the far side of the barangay we had visited earlier. The church had arranged for me to speak at their crusade in the middle of this shanty town. There was a courtyard sometimes used for basketball and the musicians had set up ready. Hundreds of people turned out to the square for the meeting. It was easy to imagine Jesus speaking in such a situation. I could imagine in this crowd, the four men climbing onto the roof, breaking it open and lowering their crippled friend down to Jesus to be healed.

As the musicians struck up their first song, a large rat skipped over my feet chased by a flea-bitten cat. Leaping over the musicians' guitar cases, the rat disappeared into the darkness. Over two hundred people gathered. More were expected but there was rain in the air. The children were fascinated with us and stroked our hair.

The whole meeting was in Ilongo, the local Filipino language. There were a few songs in English but all the testimonies and announcements were in

Ilongo. I was called forward to preach and Pastor Ed interpreted. Speaking through an interpreter into a culture which is unfamiliar was quite an experience. As I closed my message torrential rain covered the area and people scattered into houses. We were escorted into someone's house where a western-style settee – the only piece of western furniture I had seen – was standing on a couple of boxes to protect it from the expected flood. Here there was a television and a stereo system. This, I was told, was middle class. I suppose compared to the bamboo houses on the beach it had something to commend it. Yet this house too, stood by an open sewer, infested by rats, cockroaches and other disease-spreading life forms.

When the rain stopped, we made our way into the darkness to find a taxi on the main road. On our return to Ed's place, two large cockroaches welcomed us and ran up the wall. I found it hard to relax as we sat to eat supper. For supper Dottie had pigs' intestines, Ed ate the pigs' brains and rice, Jireh had red sausages made from cultured worms. Mercifully there were two pieces of what looked like fried chicken for Kerry and me. A few french fries appeared and I tried to imagine for a moment that I was somewhere else eating chicken and chips.

We turned in for bed with a 6am start ahead of us. The prospect of sleeping in the dark with so much wildlife wandering about filled me with dread. I was incredibly jumpy. Perhaps tomorrow would be better.

After lying awake all night, we had an early start with the weekly prayer breakfast at the church centre. Pigs' intestine soup didn't seem too appetising at 7am so I stuck to coffee and dry bread.

The testimonies were all in Ilongo but one of them needed no interpretation. It was clearly about a couple of Westerners encountering a bamboo bridge. Whatever he was saying they found it very funny.

After breakfast hundreds of children, from the Helping Hands sponsorship scheme, streamed into the building. Worship was led by Dottie and Alen, a church worker who lived with Ed and Dottie. Then we taught them an action chorus in English before they split up into groups for teaching.

For sometime, Ed and the other pastors had been pleading with me to stay with them for the week instead of going with Wendy and Kerry to Mindanao on Monday. I was falling in love with these people yet still a little anxious at the thought of being here alone. We went to the airport to confirm our flights for the coming Monday but I decided to rearrange my flight for one week later and stay here in Iloilo, to be the main speaker at the three-day pastors' convention. We got brave and took a five-mile taxi trip to the airport unaccompanied.

Ed and Dottie were now very busy with preparations for the church's eighth anniversary next day, so we made a visit to Dunkin' Doughnuts to cool off.

We ventured into a department store and I found a T-shirt with the slogan 'I survived Iloilo'. It was made for me. I had yet to survive Iloilo for sure but I bought it in faith that God would bring me through this amazing experience.

In the afternoon we went to change some money and do a few practical things. After a white-knuckle ride in an horrendous taxi, we arrived home in the darkness and fell into bed, hardly bothering about possible visits from the insect world.

On the Sunday, waking after a good night's sleep we found we were in the middle of a blackout. Having received a new confidence from on high, I stepped boldly into the shower without the usual shoe-throwing ritual, and in my best Clint Eastwood voice said, "Go ahead cockroach, make my day!"

Having showered in ice-cold water, we emerged from our room to a wonderful breakfast of fried eggs, sweet bread and coffee. An English breakfast was on the table. God was in his heaven and all was well with the world. All was well at the power station too – the electricity came back on.

We caught a jeepney into town and the service began. About five hundred people came and this was only part of the church. Many meet in smaller groups out in the barangays with the local pastors. Wendy sang a solo. They began applauding as she began to sing – they are so encouraging. Kerry preached with Ed interpreting. Everyone was in their best clothes.

Pastors from some of the churches planted on the other islands joined us in preparation for the convention. The service lasted for over five hours but seemed much less. I confirmed to Ed that I would not leave with the others in the morning but would stay on and speak at the pastors' convention. Ed was very pleased at this news and announced it to the sound of more applause.

At teatime a whole pig was brought in on a bamboo pole. Stuffed with banana-leaves, it had been roasted over an open fire. As guest of honour I was given the privilege of cutting off the pig's head so the feast could begin. Though not very big, this pig was meant to feed all 500 guests.

After everyone had eaten and the tables were cleared away there was another service. The evening service featured an address by the city mayor and some special musical items, including a choir and me as the preacher.

I stood to preach and paused for a moment. I looked out over the crowd. I looked out of the window, across the city rooftops. Looking at faces in the crowd I asked myself, "What is the most important message to share right now?" I explained again the timeless story of the God who made the world and created us – every race – in his own image because he wanted a relationship with us. I told of his broken heart as man turned his back on God. I explained the gracious rescue plan of God, who sent his own Son to the world, who took our place under judgement, died for us and rose again for us, overcoming the power of death. I told them that this Jesus was present with us and ready to receive those wanting to be restored to a relationship with their Father and Creator.

About fifty people responded and stood with me at the front of the church as I led them in a simple prayer to receive Jesus into their hearts. I told of the healing power of Jesus and many came for prayer for healing. The room was hot and humid but also pregnant with God's presence.

When it was all over, we were sung to and showered with gifts from people who we knew could ill afford them. This display of Filipino love for us, convinced me it was right to stay on here when the Kerry and Wendy left tomorrow.

On the Monday Kerry left at 4.30am with Ed on his motorbike and sidecar, for his flight to the southern island of Mindanao. Too exhausted to move, I stayed in bed and tried to get some sleep. As the sound of the motorbike faded into the distance I realised that I had developed a chest infection and that one of my insect bites was beginning to swell up. Kerry had just left with my medical insurance. I had no way of contacting him in an emergency. I prayed.

All alone, apart from my new Filipino friends, I spent a week with church leaders, pastors and evangelists. I was the main speaker for this conference and the other speaker did not arrive. I ended up speaking three or four times a day with an evangelistic meeting each evening.

The days slipped by and God gave me peace and grace to be there alone. The conference had some great moments as we really connected together in the Spirit.

The first night sleeping alone at Ed's house, I reached into a cupboard to get my Bible. As I did, a large four-inch cockroach dropped onto the back of my hand and hissed at me. I shook it off and jumped on the bed and under the mosquito net and watched it walk under the wardrobe. It was not the experience I needed just before turning out the light. Part of me prayed that this whole experience would be over sooner rather than later. I didn't sleep much that night.

The week soon passed and the conference ended and I shared the farewells with all the pastors as they went their separate ways.

On Saturday, I travelled with Ed and Dottie to the Island of Negros, to Bacolod City where Ed's brother was pastor of a small church. The old rusty white ferry sat at an angle in the water, as though leaning on the quay to rest its weary frame. Several holes were visible in its side as we boarded. We found a seat in the shade on the open deck. A rat scurried away as the crowds boarded. As the journey got under way, I walked round the deck. I looked out across the ocean at the many islands lined with palm trees. I felt a breeze in the air which was a welcome break in the constant heat and humidity. I was full of wonder that God had brought me here. I felt strange for a moment. I was standing in my destiny – to be an 'apostle' – one who is 'sent' by God.

The following morning, about two hundred people gathered in a small scout hut. I was treated like a visiting president. The poverty seemed even more acute here. Some of the women had brought food – but it was only for us visitors.

As I stood to preach, again I looked into the eyes of the poor. I opened my mouth to begin but this time tears came instead. I regained my composure and told of the love and mercy of Jesus. Five people came and stood with me to ask Jesus into their hearts. I cannot communicate the immense privilege I felt to be there that morning.

Later, we said our farewells on the quayside as we boarded the ferry back to Iloilo. We arrived back at Ed's place in darkness and I had to pack. I needed to get ready to leave early in the morning, to join Kerry and Wendy in Osamiz City on the Island of Mindanao – the Islamic militant stronghold of the Philippines. An American Bible translator was currently being held hostage there. The conditions of his release were that no more western missionaries were to be allowed onto Mindanao.

Chapter 12

The blind man and the awkward turkey

At 4 am Ed took me to the airport on the motorbike
and sidecar but enlisted the driving skills of Pastor
Celso Galvez, who had been a good friend to me
during my stay. We boarded the plane for Cebu
Island and the flight took just under an hour. We had
quite a wait in Cebu and then caught a small, fifty-
seater plane, to the Island of Mindanao and Osamiz
City.

Here I encountered another overwhelming
Filipino welcome with garlands of flowers, singing,
and the impression they were greeting a hero or
some long-lost friend. It was good to see Kerry and
Wendy again.

Here, the Happy Church was a little more
established than Ed's church and they had their own
building and their own jeep.

Pastor Elvie Go was the senior pastor here. She
was a single woman with an infectious laugh. Also
Pastor James introduced himself, a single Filipino
about my own age.

After I settled in, they took us to the beach. It
was a ride away from the poverty to palm trees
and an empty beach. They broke open the food –
roast chicken and roast potatoes – Kerry obviously
realised I would have been struggling with the food

in Iloilo. We even went for a swim in the warm sea. It was so hot we were virtually dry before we got back to the House of Mercy, our accommodation for the night. There was a theological college, primary school, doctor's surgery and other facilities, as well as accommodation for visitors.

Kerry and Wendy spoiled me by arranging to have roast beef and Yorkshire pudding for supper. They invited the Filipinos to try some English cuisine. It was funny to see that they were as hesitant about English food as I was about Filipino food. They were horrified that there was no rice!

As we prepared for bed, I discovered that I had brought a cockroach with me in my luggage. Kerry and I had fun chasing it round the bedroom. We never caught it but, this being a brick building, there was much less of a problem with unwelcome visitors in the night – and no gecko!

In the morning we were assigned to the training centre and gave three lectures and a practical on the baptism of the Holy Spirit to the workers of the Happy Church. It seemed odd that God should use a couple of Anglicans from reserved England to come and teach Pentecostal Filipinos about the gifts of the Holy Spirit!

After lunch we drove some distance in the jeep to a remote jungle area for a crusade. When we arrived the Happy Church music group were in full swing. A crowd of about three hundred people had gathered – all non-Christians. Wendy sang a solo and then Pastor Elvie announced, "Brother Don will now sing."

When Kerry and Wendy had finished laughing, we did a song together, much to my relief! Then Kerry preached.

At the close of his message, most of the people came forward to receive Christ. By the time 129 names had been taken it was going dark and people were beginning to disperse, so we missed some.

A man who was blind came forward and Kerry and I were asked to pray that he might see. The first time we prayed he said he could see lights but not make out people's faces. Then we prayed again and he said, rather matter-of-factly, "I can see." I couldn't really believe it at the time but, visiting the country some years later, Pastor Elvie told me he could still see and his life had changed completely.

We met the local pastor of this outreach and his wife. Before this afternoon there wasn't really a church there to speak of – just seven Christians. Now they had at least one hundred and twenty-nine Christians, not including the children who responded.

On the way back we travelled in the coach with the music group. There were many shouts of "Dalyaawen ang Dios!" (Praises to God.)

In the evening I spoke at the Happy House Bible study to about fifty people. I wore a barong, the national dress, and it caused a bit of a stir. Good fun.

Afterwards we met the Australians who were there for a few weeks to build a house for a family, whose house was falling down and beyond repair.

Next morning I met the children of Bethesda, the House of Mercy. They all came from difficult situations or even off the street. They were aged about five years and under. They were very funny and very loving. One of the boys had a shaved head and scars all over his head, which concerned me. When I asked the ladies who looked after the children, they explained that this four-year-old was sleeping on the streets and, in the night, rats would come and bite him. He had been abandoned by his family because they were too poor to care for him.

Later we went on the weekly trip to the city hospital to pray for the sick. I use the term hospital loosely. It was as rundown as most buildings there and even more infested with cockroaches. Many beds had no mattress, so the sick were laid onto the metal springs. Occasionally, a thin palm mat served as a mattress.

In the most harrowing room, a lady in her fifties lay dying of breast cancer. There was no prospect of an operation or therapy. Painkillers were her only medication. She had no mattress on her bed and one of the bed's legs was missing, so one corner of the bed stood on some bricks and lumps of concrete.

Dena, who was our guide, asked if Wendy would sing for this lady. As Wendy bravely knelt by this lady's bed and sang, 'Such love', I found it all too much. Not only the horror and hellishness of this place, but somehow just by our simple obedience to come here, Jesus was here in a special way. In Wendy's expression of love, and the words of that beautiful song, Jesus was kneeling at this woman's bedside.

Dena then led the lady in a prayer of commitment to Christ. In a few days this lady would see the face of Jesus more clearly. What was expressed now through us, very dimly, soon she would see face to face in Christ.

As we left that terrible place Dena, who had been so positive and whose smile warmed each room there, suddenly faltered and said, "I don't like hospitals. I hate what Satan is doing to these people." I realised that though Dena was a regular visitor here, this was no easier for her than it was for us.

In stark contrast to the hospital, after the weekly prayer meeting, we were taken for ice-cream. Kerry and I were struck by the menu on the wall listing the various flavours. At the bottom of the list it read 'Live Turkey'. We weren't sure if this was a flavour of ice-cream or a sideline of the owner. It turned out that, as well as ice-cream, one could actually buy a live turkey!

Kerry was so impressed with this option, he bought it as a house-warming present for the family the Australians had built a new house for. We were about to go to the dedication of the house.

As we got into the truck to leave the ice-cream parlour, Kerry got back out for something and left me in charge of the turkey. A little disturbed at having its feet tied, the turkey decided to make a break for freedom. Suddenly, I was fighting with an outraged turkey on the floor of the truck as Wendy fell about laughing. It took Kerry and me several minutes to regain control of the turkey before we set off for the house dedication.

The house was out in a remote barangay in jungle surroundings. It comprised a single room about ten feet by ten feet, with a tiny kitchen area of about three feet by six feet. There was no electricity or water supply. As night fell, they lit the house with home-made oil lamps – medicine bottles filled with paraffin with a newspaper wick.

After the Australian dedication, Kerry presented the owner with the live turkey, much to her delight. We returned to the Happy House where a whole pig was presented for supper on account of it being the Australians' last night there.

We three English folk walked back to Bethesda, where we were staying, accompanied, as usual, by Mary who looked after us during our stay. Next day I preached to the elderly, who congregated every day for a Bible study.

In the afternoon we visited the house the Australians built so we could see it in daylight and assess if this was a possible type of project we should get involved in. The journey there was in a motorbike and sidecar – seven of us squeezed in. We reached top speeds of an incredible twelve miles an hour. We reached the jungle area and were reunited with the house owner and the awkward turkey, which glared at us when we arrived. A young man was sent up a tree with a machete and shortly afterwards several large coconuts crashed to the ground for us to drink from.

Next day, during the farewell meal, over thirty people from the Happy House came in to sing a farewell to us. Being the loving Filipinos they were, this took about half an hour. Wendy, not fond of long goodbyes, struggled a little. And even Pastor Elvie said her eyes were perspiring! Kerry and I struggled to maintain a British stiff upper lip.

After supper they all came with us to the overnight ferry to see us off. Another long goodbye ensued. The ferry would take us to Cebu Island and from there we would make our way to Manila by air. Although we had a cabin to sleep in, a few cockroaches decided to join us which, for me at least, made the night a rather long one.

As we touched down on British soil, only God knew the gratitude in my heart at our safe return. The peaceful order of the plane was disturbed momentarily, as three English people cheered and shouted "Salamat sa Dios!" (Thanks be to God!), as we landed. We were met by our respective spouses and it was so good to see Hazel and the girls again. It was so good to feel cold too.

As we made our way home through the English December chill, the events of the last three weeks seemed like a dream. Had we really just been to the ends of the earth? And, more disturbingly, what had God got for us next?

Chapter 13

The Fellowship of the King

The trip to Asia was a tipping point in my life. For months, if not years, I had been thinking of what life might be like if I could be freed from the duties of parish ministry. I had begun writing down what an itinerant ministry might look like for me and how I might bring it about. It struck me that all our evangelism was in partnership with other Christians, either on the team or in whose church we ministered. We were doing evangelism in fellowship with other Christians. I began to formulate ideas for a ministry called The Evangelism Fellowship, assuming that Kerry and I would work increasingly together.

It was about this time that Kerry invited me to join him on the 'Arrow Retreat' for evangelists, at St John's Theological College in Nottingham, hosted by the evangelist J. John. The main speaker at the retreat was Paul Stanley, vice-president of the Navigators, who taught us about the three stages of life and how to develop our ministry and how to 'finish well'. The point was to narrow down what we do to one or two things – to be sharp in one area rather than blunt in many. The retreat was a breath of fresh air and convinced me I could work towards an independently financed ministry.

The subsequent invitations to this retreat have kept me stable and hopeful over the years, particularly in times of adversity. Fellowship with other evangelists is something I value immensely. They are the Fellowship of the King, as we all play our part in the quest of God to rescue mankind from the kingdom of darkness.

That year was one where I began to feel pulled in opposite directions. All the usual activity of a busy parish carried on unabated. There was a major stewardship campaign at St Peter's called Firstfruits where the whole congregation was surveyed about their time and talents and what part they wanted to play in the church. There were PCC meetings, deanery and clergy meetings, Churches Together meetings and the spire was put back on the church tower. But increasingly, these things meant little to me as I focussed on the task of evangelism.

Luis Palau was speaking at a crusade in Luton that year and I went over just to watch a master at work. I had followed Luis' ministry since I read his autobiography back in the 1970s. Thousands came to hear him, many in overflow rooms. I managed to get a seat at the side near the platform. Watching how he appealed to people to give their life to Christ and seeing people come forward was very moving. It inspired me to focus on communicating the gospel.

Also that year, Kerry and I were invited to be part of a team of evangelists on a Church Army mission to a group of Anglican churches in Newmarket. These missions often ended up being a mission to the church congregation rather than impacting the community at large. However, we gave it our best shot and met many wonderful people and saw people commit their life to Jesus Christ and the church encouraged.

Kerry was planning a mission in his church, over at Hemingford Grey, near Cambridge. Following on from the successes and strengths of RSVP '93, he began to develop a mission strategy for a week of events called RSVP '94 and invited me to speak at the main meetings.

This opportunity came at one of the most difficult times of my ministry. I was fast approaching the end of my five-year contract at Stowmarket. I knew I couldn't go on in parish ministry – I was obviously a round peg in a square hole. Yet the idea of how I might launch out full-time, into an itinerant ministry, was far from being fully formed. The grief of the past decade had also resurfaced and I was feeling increasingly burnt-out.

I had gathered a few friends together and formed a charity called The Evangelism Fellowship. People were beginning to give a little towards the vision and, for integrity, we needed a charity to hold funds for mission.

The RSVP '94 mission turned out to be a series of dinners at which I was the after-dinner speaker. Most were held in a hotel in St Ives and were themed dinners such as jazz and dine, classical concert and dinner, a barn dance and a gospel concert in a theatre.

I arrived at the mission with my spiritual fuel tank running on empty. I had nothing left to give.

I threw myself on the mercy of God day and night. All I had was my testimony – the story of what Jesus had done in my life. Like Saint Paul, "I didn't come with wise and persuasive words" but was hoping for a "demonstration of the Spirit's power". At one of the greatest speaking opportunities in my ministry, I felt I had little to say.

At the 'Jazz and Dine' event, I sat opposite a Jewish lady who told me she hated religion. Her father was very religious and she hated religion. Did I mention... she hated religion? She particularly hated "those people you end up sitting next to who want to get you saved". I decided to put my cards on the table. I told her that not only was I one of those people that wanted to get everyone 'saved' but, in about ten minutes time, I was about to do that very thing. I said I would be interested to know if I had managed to do it in a way that didn't put her off.

I stood as I shared my story with those gathered and told how Jesus had come into my life and changed everything. I spoke of the wonderful peace I encountered as I said 'Yes' to Jesus, how clean I felt inside. I led people in a prayer to receive Christ and handed back to Kerry.

My Jewish friend was quieter. After an awkward silence she shared some of her spiritual ideas which were greatly influenced by New Age thinking. Something must have happened though because she came back to events later in the week and brought a friend with her.

Just before the mission started, I had received a

letter from an African who was in England for the first time, visiting from Uganda. He was writing from London, asking if he could join us in the mission as he was an evangelist. I'm normally suspicious of such letters from complete strangers but, on this occasion, I felt the Holy Spirit tell me to welcome this man because my future was tied up with his future. I wrote and told Charles Mugisha he would be most welcome as part of the mission team. I also wrote that, if he had any time after the mission, he could come over to Stowmarket and spend some time with us there.

Every day on RSVP '94 the team had lunch together at the church rooms in Hemingford Grey. It was over these lunches that I became friends with Charles and he talked of his home church in Gaba, Uganda. The trip to the Philippines had created in me a new fascination with cultures and we talked about the Philippines and Uganda every lunchtime. Charles suggested that as we had visited the Philippines, Kerry and I should visit him in Uganda. The idea seemed a complete fantasy – we didn't have any finance to do such things. We started by joking about us going out to Uganda but, by the end of the mission week, we had discussed quite a lot of details about a possible trip to Uganda. We were left with a serious decision to be made. It seemed ludicrous to be thinking about such a trip as my contract was coming to an end in Stowmarket and the future looked quite uncertain.

Charles came to stay with us in Stowmarket for a

couple of weeks and we shared testimony and vision every evening. We went into schools to do assemblies and Charles preached at several churches including St Peter's in Stowmarket. This visit really developed our friendship and, as Charles was leaving to return home, I asked about what he would do when he got back. It transpired that he had given up his job to come to England. His home really went with the job, so he was unsure what would happen on his return. A few people in our congregation really felt we should support Charles as he developed his vision for ministry. The Evangelism Fellowship agreed to set up a fund called The Uganda Partnership to develop this relationship with Charles and to help support his ministry. A small group of supporters gave monthly donations and we transferred funds to Charles out in Uganda.

With the help of Catherine Wellingbrook, the Regional Director from Church Army, I devised a plan to phase out my employment with the diocese and phase in independent funding through the Trust. My secret hope was that the diocese would let us continue to live in the church house in Stowmarket, as they had already decided that I would not be replaced when I went. So the house would not be needed for anyone else.

The diocese was without a bishop at the time, so I went to see the suffragan Bishop of Dunwich – a strange title, as most of Dunwich had long since disappeared into the sea. I put my ideas to the bishop and found that money speaks louder than words. I was offering to take a 25 per cent pay cut in return for having 25 per cent of the year to develop the itinerant ministry and the Evangelism Fellowship. The offer of costing the diocese 25 per cent less was obviously attractive to the bishop as he accepted the idea. He did point out that it was a very high-risk strategy and that I may end up with nothing. I was restless with the current situation and said I would take the risk.

Technically, I was supposed to give 75 per cent of my time to the parish and 25 per cent to developing The Evangelism Fellowship. However, as is common with split-working, both jobs demanded 100 per cent of my attention. For the next four years I felt in limbo. I was, in some ways, in a worse position than before.

However, I pressed on, trying to keep the gospel at the top of the agenda. I was contacted by the Billy Graham organisation about Global Mission with Billy Graham. The idea was that Billy Graham would preach at a crusade and the meetings would be beamed by satellite all over the world. It seemed no one else in the area was bothering to get the link into Stowmarket, so I signed up as the local organiser.

The worst obstacle was the overwhelming apathy in the local churches. It seemed to me we were about to miss an historic opportunity. I hired the local cinema and arranged for someone to receive the satellite signal. These things are all much easier now but then it was difficult to find people with the necessary equipment to download the signal and also project a video picture in the cinema. It has to be said that the cinema was not packed out every night. There was more apathy it seemed. However, people did come to the mission and some did come and put their trust in Christ and for that, it was worth the effort. I did receive a couple of letters from people who had been at the 1955 Haringey meetings with Billy Graham who thanked me for giving people in the area the opportunity to see Billy Graham and encouraged me in the ministry.

Chapter 14

The pearl of Africa

As we descended through low cloud, over Lake Victoria, I caught my first sight of Africa. It was raining! I don't know what I was expecting, but it certainly wasn't rain. We landed at Entebbe and were greeted by Charles and his infectious African smile. As we drove out of the airport I looked across to the old Entebbe airport where a burnt-out 747 lay crippled on the runway, left over from the dark days of Idi Amin and the raid on Entebbe. But now, President Yoweri Museveni had been in power for thirteen years and Uganda had enjoyed relative peace, although war continued on the Northern borders with 'The Lord's Resistance Army' or LRA.

Uganda was in a time of Christian revival. There was immense freedom for preaching the gospel everywhere. Even on the state radio station, people gave their testimonies and recommended Jesus. As we made the one-hour journey to Kampala, I couldn't help noticing the white recycled Toyotas that made up ninety percent of the traffic.

We passed through Kampala and made our way out to Lake Victoria, to the village of Gaba, a trading centre on the shores of the Lake.

We were taken to the home of Pastor Peter Kasirivu where we would stay during the trip.

The ladies of the house had prepared for us an amazing meal of fish and chips. I suspect this was at Charles' suggestion, as we had shared fish and chips on his first night with us in Stowmarket. It was a welcome relief from the usual culture shock one faces when visiting the Third World.

Kerry had a vision to bring out ten young people to have an African experience the following year, so our main task was to see if this was viable.

It was great to meet Pastor Peter, as Charles had told us so much about him. We chatted all afternoon and then darkness fell. We set up our mosquito nets and prepared for bed. As I got under the net and began tucking it into the mattress in my usual paranoid way, Kerry began laughing and saying, "I can't do it! I can't do it!"

"Can't do what?" I asked.

"I've put a plastic snake in your bed," he confessed.

Jumpy as ever about being in a strange country, the last thing I needed was to find a snake, plastic or otherwise, in my bed. This incident may explain why we no longer do missions together any more.

The following morning we told the story to our hosts who had mixed reactions. Charles, however, found it very amusing. After showing us around Gaba and the church we went to his house. He placed the plastic snake in the middle of the floor and began calling to his neighbour. A small but formidable African lady came in with a sweeping brush and began attacking the snake. The noise attracted a group of local children who came to look. Everyone was shouting but Charles was laughing at the spectacle. Eventually he told them the truth and the snake was examined.

The children, who sadly don't have toys, were fascinated with the toy snake. They asked if they could have it and we agreed. They ran off and wreaked havoc throughout the village. They would walk up to a house, throw the snake through an open window and watch the occupants flee the house screaming. They then retrieved the snake and went to another house and repeated the prank. I wasn't entirely sure we were being a blessing to the people of the village.

Gaba Church, back then, met in an old tent. They had land but no building. An evangelist had retired and given them his crusade tent for a place to meet. Out of this tent the community was helped and blessed. There was a thriving feeding programme and we watched on Saturday morning as hundreds of the village children streamed into church to be fed. At that time, Uganda had the worst AIDS problem in the world and thousands of children were being orphaned. Lack of education was aggravating the problem as it was commonly believed that condoms caused AIDS. It was also believed that if you caught HIV you could be cured by sexual intercourse with a virgin. The younger she was the more likely you would be cured. As you can imagine, this ignorance made the problem far worse.

Not surprising therefore, was Gaba's ministry in education where Revd Nathan Amooti was head of a thriving but struggling primary school, Maranatha Academy. Hundreds of children, many sponsored, received an education to give them a far better start in life than many of their parents had.

On Sunday morning we joined Charles and Peter at their church service in the tent and I had the privilege of preaching. About ten people came and put their trust in Jesus and some came forward for healing.

For me, the worship stands out in my memory and the young people who led it. Not least was the leader, a girl named Grace. Grace was, indeed, amazing.

Kerry and I also had the privilege of preaching at the lunch-hour fellowship at the Trumpet Centre, in Kampala, hosted by Revd John Mulinde. We didn't know it at the time, but John would also come and visit us in England with a powerful message from God.

We preached in various schools and met Charles' younger brother, Fred Katagwa, who introduced us to the Christian Union at his school. We also toured the city and Charles took us to Namugongo, the shrine of the first Ugandan martyrs. The shrine is about twenty minutes drive from Kampala. Christianity was foreign to the people living in this heart of Africa until the 1800s when it left forever a mark at Namugongo and on the life of Africa. A spot inside the church, at Namugongo, marks where the brutal murder of twenty-six Christians took place by agents of Kabaka (king) Mwanga of Buganda.

The crime of the converts was that they defied their kabaka and would prefer attending Sunday church service instead of meeting the king's social needs. Illiterate subjects, some barely a week old in the Christian faith, laid down their lives for what they believed in. This was to forsake life principles and values held for the greater part of their lifetime and that of their forefathers. It was unheard of for a page to reject the wishes of a king.

What followed was the execution to restore the authority of the king that had been challenged. Some Christians were picked from Munyonyo and were murdered along the way. Others made it to Namugongo, Kabaka Mwanga's execution centre. Here the young men were bound and thrown on a fire. Burnt alive, as a warning to others who thought they might refuse the king.

Kabaka Mwanga's plan backfired though, as the Christians' martyrdom set the foundation of Christianity in the Buganda kingdom. Christianity eventually became dominant in other parts of Uganda. The shrine was built to honour the martyrs.

We also visited Namirembe Cathedral in Kampala and, here too, were graves of people who had laid down their lives for the gospel. One grave marked the resting place of an English missionary, his last words were written on the headstone. "Tell the Kabaka – I died for Uganda."

It made me realise how easy it was for us to follow in the footsteps of the first missionaries to this continent. They had sown in tears. We now reaped in joy. As Tertullian said, "The blood of the martyrs is the seed of the church."

Very early next morning, before the dazzling African sun had climbed into a cloudless sky, Charles collected us from Peter's house and we caught a taxi into Kampala to catch the early morning coach to Kenya. We had been asked by a friend if we could visit the widow of a pastor in Nakuru, in neighbouring Kenya. Our friend wanted to help with an orphanage for street children but, since the pastor had died, he had not been able to communicate with his widow. He wanted to know if there was an orphanage or if there could be, if money was raised.

We climbed aboard the huge Isuzu coach in the centre of Kampala. It was crammed full with people and luggage. A few goats and chickens bleated and clucked their objection to the cramped conditions, as we made our way on the long journey to Kenya. Bizarrely, there was an onboard video of the story of Michael Jackson, as we raced towards the border. At various villages along the way, the coach pulled over and various items of food, including small bags of fried locust, were offered for sale through the open windows.

At the border we experienced another clash of

cultures. As a child it had always been drummed into me that it is polite to queue and quite rude to push in or jump the queue. What was hard for Kerry and me to grasp was that queuing is a quintessentially British tradition. As we went to see the immigration officer to get our passport stamped, to get access to Kenya, there were many people waiting to see him. In typical English fashion, Kerry and I formed a queue. The problem was, no one else joined us. Every time the office door opened, everyone rushed the door. But still we queued. It was so hard to just join the scrum and push past like everyone else. After an hour of this frustration we did eventually rush the door and get in. When in Rome...

On the other side of the border, many people with leprosy, with hands and fingers missing, begged for money through the window of the bus. We pressed on, through the heat, into Western Kenya. We stopped for an hour for lunch, in Kisumu, and we continued to chat with Charles who was now, like us, a stranger in a foreign land. After lunch and a walk, we returned to the coach to complete this exhausting journey.

After what seemed like hours, we finally arrived in Nakuru, where we were met by Catherine, the widow of the pastor our friend had been writing to. She took us to her home and gave us food and drink. She lived in a small house in a slum area with her three children and I wondered where the three of us would stay, ever anxious about where we would sleep.

Charles stayed with Catherine, and Kerry and I were taken to meet 'Auntie May'. Auntie May was an old white-haired lady, originally from Sierra Leone, and had been married to an Englishman until he died some years before. She lived in a small house but owned another house nearby, she told us, where she housed visitors from time to time. It seemed we would have our own place. She walked us down to the property, which was actually a derelict house with no electricity and faulty plumbing. Mercifully there was a flush toilet and we were spared the nightmare of the 'long-drop'. The toilet had an interesting flush. When the chain was pulled, the water overflowed from the high-level cistern all over the floor. It made a better shower than a toilet.

The house was empty, except for an old bed in the corner of one room. By this time, I was feeling highly stressed and well out of my depth. Kerry very graciously offered me the bed and slept on the floor. Brave man.

As we switched off the torch for the night, I listened in the darkness to the sound of African crickets, and wondered what I was doing here in 'darkest Africa'.

Next morning, we woke early after a difficult night. We emerged into the Kenyan sunshine and walked up to Auntie May's house. She had prepared a full English breakfast for us which was a real blessing.

"My husband used to like this," she told us.

As we finished our breakfast, Catherine and Charles arrived and we went into the city. Catherine explained that there wasn't an orphanage but the problem of street children was a growing one. Sometimes she had taken one or two into her own home. Her husband had had a vision to raise money for a home but now he was gone. The trip had achieved what was intended in that it had clarified the situation for our friend. But it seemed a long way to come to find nothing. We spent the day talking with Catherine until the night descended once again.

A large African moon sat in the sky as Kerry and I made our way, through the back streets, to Auntie May's. After coffee with Auntie May, we walked down through the shadows to our digs. We slept better but had to be up early for the long journey back to Uganda. The coach was always overbooked and would be full by the time it got to Nakuru, so Catherine took us to a taxi park and negotiated a fare with a man in a Peugeot.

The cheapest form of transport was the dreaded Kenyan 'matatu'. A matatu can really be any vehicle but is usually a small van into which more people than can really fit are squeezed into the back to maximise the fares of the owner. Kenyans tell me 'matatu' is the Kiswahili word for 'three' and means that a matatu holds three times more people than it should.

Catherine told the man with the Peugeot, that we were not, under any circumstances to be transferred to a matatu. The man nodded agreeingly. At the first town we arrived at, he transferred us to a matatu – like lambs to the slaughter. Being crammed into the back of a very small van with thirty other people is bad enough. Knowing, as feeling disappears from your legs, that you are going to be this cramped for about five hours is much worse. Matatu drivers are also infamous for dangerous driving. So it's hard to know which is worse – the speed or being crushed.

At the matatu park where we stopped briefly, some matatu drivers were honest in their advertising. One matatu had '100 per cent pure pain' written on the side of it. Another had, 'Pain without compromise'.

At the border with Uganda we abandoned the matatu and treated ourselves to the comparative luxury of a Ugandan minibus. At least here it was one person to a seat instead of three or four. We breathed a sigh of relief as we returned to Peter's house.

Our last task for this fact-finding trip was to visit Uganda's national park, to see if it would be viable to bring a large group of young people on safari, if next year's trip went ahead. We travelled with Charles and his friend James, in James' little Suzuki jeep, south towards the border with Rwanda, to Uganda's national park.

Mweya Safari Lodge sits on a peninsula within the heart of the spectacular Queen Elizabeth National Park, with breathtaking views of the lakes and miles of unspoilt savannah. We arrived as the sun was resting on the horizon, painting amazing sunsets in the sky. We checked into our rooms and then went for dinner.

What surprised me was that the hotel did not have a fence round it. So all the wildlife could walk up to the hotel. Added to this, our rooms were not down an internal corridor but a walk across the car park outside. So after dinner we walked nervously back to our rooms. The slightest interruption to the rhythm of the sound of crickets made Kerry and me jump. We got to our room and said goodnight to Charles and James. We closed the door and made sure it was firmly closed. We set up our mosquito nets and got into bed, reflecting on the long journey here. Kerry and I chatted for a while and watched a number of small lizards gathered round the light. We turned out the light and slept well.

The following morning we left at sunrise to go on a safari for two hours, seeing herds of Uganda's animals in their natural habitat – impala and hyenas, elephants and baboons.

We returned to the hotel and took our breakfast out on the veranda, where a buffet of cornflakes and full English breakfast was on offer, along with various African dishes and excellent coffee. I can't imagine the Garden of Eden being much more stunning than this. It was idyllic. The sunshine, the wildlife, stunning views of the lakes, the birdsong and the wonderful food. A warthog wandered across the lawn as we ate. It was one of those moments one doesn't want to end.

In the afternoon we took a boat out onto the lake and saw hundreds of hippos swimming and a large herd of elephants coming down to the lake to drink. What a privilege to be there.

We made the long journey back to Kampala and spent the next day visiting craft markets in the centre of Kampala to get a few souvenirs. Our mission complete, we said our farewells and left for Entebbe and the flight back to England.

Later that year, Kerry and I returned to the Philippines, on a four-week mission with two teams of ten people. Andy and Wendy Diaper led a team to Mindanao and I led a team to Iloilo. Kerry planned to spend the first two weeks with my team and then join the Diapers on Mindanao.

There were many frustrations in the team and in some ways, it was just too big a team. The men all slept in one room of the church on the floor. The church building was visited by large rats and cockroaches so this was a challenge. The women shared some rooms at the other end of the church offices. Putting twelve people of very different personalities in cramped conditions and depriving them of all that is familiar is a recipe for conflict. Television producers base TV programmes on the idea – so-called reality TV.

The task we faced was to build houses for the poor. But when we arrived, land had not been identified, let alone purchased. So we had a team with little to do for two weeks, all becoming irritable.

At the end of the first two weeks, Kerry left for Mindanao. Two days later, I got a call from Andy, the team leader there, to tell me that Kerry had become very sick and had caught a flight back home. I was shocked because I had been relying on Kerry to help me get the team back to Manila and on the plane home. I had no experience of leading teams overseas and had only agreed to this arrangement on the understanding that he would come back towards the end of the trip to organise the internal flights and the night we would have to spend in Manila. But nothing could be done. He was very sick and had gone home.

A couple of days later, Mandy one of the team became very ill and was admitted to hospital with stomach problems. Things seemed to be getting worse. The team had all been invited on the trip by Kerry, so there wasn't a natural sense in which I was seen as leader. This too made the mission difficult. To be honest, I was very glad when the whole thing was over and we all got home. I didn't realise it yet but I was beginning to learn that my personality doesn't really suit these large teams.

Chapter 15

The deaf boy and the temple of doom

As 1996 unfolded I sensed many changes were at
hand. The contrast between parish work and the
itinerant ministry was becoming sharper. My desire
to be completely free from parish duties dominated
my waking thoughts. By this point in the ministry,
I had conducted over five hundred funerals, taken
hundreds of school assemblies and led countless
Sunday services. I had sat in hundreds of meetings
with clergy and in too many church council meetings.
After all was said and done, there was usually a lot
more said than done.

St Peter's church building was more than five
hundred years old and there had been an ongoing
restoration work all the time I had been there. The
congregation were divided about the merits of the
restoration work but, nevertheless, it continued as
the backdrop to the rest of the life of the parish. By
1996 an ambitious programme was underway to
restore the tower and replace the spire, which had
been removed for safety reasons in the 1970s. The
cost of this work was over £1,000,000.

The evangelist in me often felt we were
rearranging the deck-chairs on the Titanic. With
hindsight though, it seems that local churches are
always a mixture of maintenance and mission. So,

alongside all the usual activity of a thriving church, there were some notable moments that year.

Out of the blue, I got a call from an old friend I had lost touch with. His name was Paul Hoyle. Paul had introduced me to the ministry of Billy Graham when I first became a Christian. We had often listened to the 'Hour of Decision' programme on Radio Luxembourg, hearing Billy Graham, and occasionally Leighton Ford, Billy Graham's brother-in-law, preach the gospel in various parts of the world.

Paul came over for a weekend to Stowmarket and invited me to speak at a lunch-hour meeting at Lloyds of London. Paul was the last person I would have imagined to be working at Lloyds as his background, before he became a Christian, had been that of a hippy. It was difficult to imagine Paul in a suit and working at Lloyds. But sure enough, a few months later, he met me in London and I preached in one of the auditoriums at the Lloyds Building.

The lectern looked presidential and the room was grand. A small group from Lloyds, about forty or so people, gathered for this lunch-time meeting. As often happens, it was really a meeting of Christians but they wanted me to be evangelistic. Preaching the gospel when you're fairly sure all your hearers already know it is a challenge. However, as I checked my spirit God seemed to confirm I should preach the gospel. At the end of the meeting, a Roman Catholic lady confessed she had never known Jesus in the personal way I had shared. Paul and I prayed with her to receive Christ personally. Sometimes I am aware that God has sent me for just one person. That day, I felt sure this was a significant step for that lady.

Another notable event that year was a visit from my friend, John Mulinde, from the Trumpet Centre in Uganda. John had asked for three seminars to share a vision he had about a 'Watchmen Intercessors Network'. Unfortunately we had a very busy programme of our own and I could only get a short preaching slot in one Sunday evening service. Not to be deterred from his mission, John gave us his vision during a three-hour sermon! The first and only three hour sermon I have ever heard. The meeting started at 6.30pm and he finished speaking after 10pm. Yet so powerful was his message, when he finished no one wanted to leave. He certainly stirred up many people to a new commitment to prayer.

Through my friendship with Kerry Dixon, I had been invited to an annual retreat hosted by the Greek evangelist, J. John. Speakers over the years included evangelist Leighton Ford and Professor Martin Saunders. The retreats were then held at Brunell Manor in Torquay. These retreats were a great encouragement and we had excellent input from Leighton Ford, J. John and others. It was here, at these retreats, that I first met Andy Economides, the man who led J. John to Christ. I had no idea at the time that we would work together in missions later on.

One year Professor Martin Saunders led us in an exercise that had a profound effect on me. I don't think it is an exaggeration to say that this exercise has kept me in the ministry and without it I may have fallen a long time ago. The retreats often looked at character and lifestyle. We had sessions on 'Finishing well'. Many people come into ministry but they don't all finish well. Many fall away through scandal – usually involving the gold, the girls or the glory – or some just give up. Billy Graham is a man who is finishing well. Decades of ministry and no scandal. No loss of faith and passion.

Martin Saunders began by asking us to imagine we were the devil. Then he asked us to write down a strategy to destroy our own ministry. So, I had to imagine I was the devil and write a strategy for destroying the ministry of Don Egan. He also said we wouldn't have to share it so we could be perfectly honest. It was a stroke of genius because it immediately pointed to the weaknesses in one's character. The second exercise was to list some policies that would protect us from that strategy we had just listed. Most of us are more vulnerable when we are on our own. One of the things I decided then was to never travel alone to ministry engagements if at all possible. I examined all the possibilities I had listed and formulated some personal rules for my own protection and more importantly, for the protection of the anointing God had given me.

A few years later, these retreats were narrowed down to about ten people and I felt very privileged to be included. The retreat became know as the Associates Retreat and I was invited to become an Associate of J. John and the Philo Trust. To this day, this annual retreat continues to be a great blessing and is a place of meeting with God and also much laughter. We need to laugh more.

In August that year, Kerry and I took a team of thirty people – ten from Stowmarket and twenty from Hemingford Grey – to Uganda. The original plan had been for a team of young people but the team turned out to be made up of people of all ages, including Rebecca, my 14 year-old-daughter. We split the teams into three groups of ten with various tasks. My team was the evangelism team and we preached at various schools and churches every day. Some of the meetings were virtually spontaneous, as the message hadn't reached the school that we were coming. At one school, after some testimonies, I stood on a chair surrounded by hundreds of teenagers and preached an evangelistic message. As always I asked people to raise their hand if they would like to receive Christ into their heart. Every day we saw twenty or thirty people give their life to Christ.

In the evenings we were sent to preach in a crusade in Kampala. The preacher who should have been speaking at the meetings that week had contracted malaria, so the team was asked to stand in for him. During that week, various team members attempted to preach the gospel and all did a good job. I spoke on several nights. One particular night Kerry and I did 'tag preaching' – taking turns to preach in the same talk. We also chained up David Usher and put him in a black sack, to illustrate how Satan had bound Adam in darkness. As Kerry told how Jesus broke the power of Satan, I pulled a release cord and the sack and chains fell from David's body.

As we prayed for the sick that night, a young girl and a young boy came forward. Both were deaf and mute. As we prayed for the girl the little boy started to speak and hear. It was a bit confusing for those of us who were praying but what great news for the boy and his family. The words on the banner across the platform, during that mission, were from Luke's gospel. It read, "He welcomed them and spoke to them about the kingdom of God, and healed those who needed healing." (Luke 9:11)

That is what we have been doing since that day – we welcome people, we speak about the Kingdom of God and we pray for those who need healing. As we follow in the footsteps of Jesus, God always manifests his power.

During the mission, all the men stayed in a house we had rented for the mission. It had no running water and only occasional electricity. The only toilet was a pit-toilet at the back of the house, just near the room where I was sleeping on the floor. There was a great deal of fear of large insects among the team and so we had purchased a spray can marked with the word 'DOOM'. In order to kill mosquitos and any other unwelcome guests, we sprayed the rooms before we went out for the evening meetings. DOOM is so toxic, that several hours need to elapse after spraying, before anyone tries to enter the room. It is so toxic, it would never be allowed on sale anywhere in Europe. And so, a catchphrase was born, recited before we went to the evening meetings every night – "DOOM that room" (said, for some bizarre reason, with a Scottish accent).

After supper, we men would all take our turn to use the pit latrine at the back of the house – a little out-house with a hole in the ground, under which a huge cesspit lay. What creatures lived down that dark hole it was best not to think about. Unfortunately for the rest of us, young Matthew Cray couldn't think of much else. He entered the shadowy inner sanctum of the pit-toilet, making a detailed inspection with his torch before he began. Just in case he found trouble, he had armed himself with a can of DOOM. To be extra sure, he thought it best to release a warning shot of DOOM into the hole in the ground. Even in small doses, DOOM is very unpleasant. At least, that's what the five cockroaches that ran out of the hole obviously thought. Disturbed by the appearance of the cockroaches, Matthew panicked and sprayed the entire contents of the can of DOOM down the hole. This made matters far worse but, as he was the last in the queue, he returned to the house and got under the safety of his mosquito net.

I, on the other hand, was trying to sleep just the other side of the locked door that backed onto the toilet. Who knows how many millions of cockroaches live down a Ugandan pit-toilet. However, they all now ran under the door, into my room, fleeing

Matthew's attack of DOOM. Kerry, sleeping on the floor beside me, was the first to notice and I heard a slapping sound in the dark. Quite sure he was not given to slapping himself in his sleep, I asked what the problem was. We switched on our torches and all over the walls and floor were more cockroaches than you'd ever want to see in one place. Several were crawling over my mosquito net. So began the long dark night of the soul. I think I passed out from exhaustion rather than falling asleep.

As we got up the following morning, the mass exodus of cockroaches was still in progress. The yard at the back of the house was covered in them. They were everywhere. A lady from the next house was beating them with a broom but fighting a losing battle. Charles arrived shortly afterwards and arranged for the toilet to be properly fumigated. Although this improved the situation eventually, it meant even more of the not-so-little blighters ran out.

It may have been this incident, or the general chaos of this mission, but I made a decision that day that it was possible to do missions in a different way to Kerry, with a smaller team and for a shorter period of time. I shared my ideas with my friend Adam Waller. We decided to do a two-man mission the following year. This was the beginning of me taking responsibility for the overseas aspect of what we were doing. I will always be grateful to Kerry for showing me the basics of organising an overseas mission but our personalities are very different and we do missions in different ways.

After a great but exhausting mission, we all returned to England having been stretched emotionally and spiritually. We returned back to Stowmarket with many stories to tell and I was glad Rebecca and I had both survived.

Shortly after we returned, Jeremy Harrold, vicar of St Peter's Stowmarket, with whom I had been working for the last seven years, retired from ministry. Earlier in the year, the work on the tower had been completed and a new spire installed. Jeremy didn't want to be remembered only for the tower restoration, and he certainly did a lot more than building work, but it did somehow crown his time at Stowmarket. Shortly after Jeremy's retirement, Trevor Jones was installed as the new vicar of Stowmarket. But that's another story.

Chapter 16

Rivers in the desert

As the new chapter at St Peter's unfolded, Trevor asked me to set up the Alpha course in Stowmarket. It was a great time and we had fifty people on the first course. It was good to speak at many of the Alpha dinners and explain the gospel to new hearers. The downside, for me, was that this new activity was generating more work in the parish and it felt like I was being dragged away from the vision God had given me. Added to that, nearly a decade of ministry had left me drained spiritually. I hadn't yet learnt how to keep topped up in my spirit or about the rhythm of life and work. I had been praying to God for some time that he would fill me again with his Holy Spirit as he had in times past. I'd been to several conferences hoping for a fresh touch from God, all to no avail.

Then I went to a New Frontiers Conference in Brighton. John Arnot, from the Toronto Airport Fellowship was the main speaker and it was interesting to hear first-hand about the controversial 'Toronto Blessing'. Also speaking at the conference was Nicky Gumble from Holy Trinity Brompton. He told the usual stories about the success of the Alpha course but then ended by saying there was an anointing available for evangelists and to come to the front if we wanted to receive it. There were over three thousand people at the conference and I was up in the balcony, but I made my way quickly down the stairs and joined hundreds of others who were going forward for prayer.

Members of the ministry team were making their way through the crowds and one man laid a hand on my shoulder and began to pray. I could feel tears welling up but I didn't want to cry just then. But I heard God saying to my spirit, "This is what you've been praying for. Let it come."

I surrendered to God and real sobbing came from somewhere deep within me. Then, as the sobbing subsided, power like electricity flowed through my body. I began shaking violently. It was like water flowing into a desert, so I cried to God for more. On and on it went, this wonderful, refreshing power flowing through me. By now I was shaking so violently that I could barely stand, such was the power of God upon me. I crashed through some empty chairs and collapsed on the floor still shaking violently. Still I cried for more. I was so thirsty for God. For what seemed more than an hour, the power of God flowed through me like a great river. Eventually, it became physically painful. When I could bear it no more, I said, "Enough God. It is enough."

As I said those words, the power stopped. But like a battery that's been in the charger overnight, I stood up fully charged with the presence of God. For days after, there seemed to be electricity flowing out of me. It was like one of those moments in the Old

Testament – like Jacob's ladder or Abraham's three visitors – when one felt one should 'build an altar there', as the Old Testament leaders did when they encountered the Living God. I now believe that God anointed me for the battle which lay ahead.

Chapter 17

Adam and the dead man

Adam Waller loves rare steak. The one he had the morning we left for Uganda was extra-rare and, to me, seemed almost raw. After a three-hour trip to Heathrow and an eight-hour flight to Uganda, he was feeling quite unwell. It could have been the anti-malarials, the flight or the rare steak. Who knows?

Adam was a real answer to prayer. Some years before I had been praying for a man who would be a companion to me both at home and on ministry trips. Adam had turned up at church and befriended Hazel and me. He was already a great blessing to me and continues to be so to this day.

The two of us were on the first Evangelism Fellowship mission to Uganda. We had done overseas trips before but always in partnership with Kerry Dixon and Signpost International. Now we were on our first independent mission to Uganda. Having only the two of us on the team simplified the arrangements and suited my temperament, much more than the thirty people we had had on the team the previous year.

After staying the first night in Uganda at Pastor Peter Kasirivu's house, Adam was very unwell. We spent the next day at Peter's house and gave Adam only medicinal drinks to rehydrate him. Gradually he came back to life.

The first week was spent preaching at a crusade in the Emperiwe district of Kampala. Charles had prepared a week-long open-air mission by the side of a busy road. Adam was given the task of videoing the mission and I was the speaker each night. Adam is also a technical wizard and greatly improved the speaker system output by removing most of the distortion, working with our friend Moses Male, the church technician.

At this time, I hadn't planned to do as much preaching as I did during that week but Charles was passionate about reaching as many people as possible with the good news of Jesus Christ. It stretched me spiritually and emotionally but I too believe that people need to repent and believe the good news or there will be hell to pay. Literally.

Every night I preached a simple message, and called people to receive Jesus Christ into their heart. Dozens responded every night. As the sun went down we prayed for the sick.

On the first night, the meeting was disturbed by a drunken man who called out and heckled during the message. The church pastor pleaded with him every night to turn from his ways and receive Christ. Every night he refused. On the fourth night, he didn't show up and people wondered where he was. Just before I preached, the pastor told the crowd that when they had come to church that morning, they had found the man lying dead on the ground, apparently having suffered alcohol poisoning or liver failure. The pastor told the crowd that none of us knows how many days we have on this earth. That the purpose of the mission was to call people to receive Christ before it is too late. For this man, who had stubbornly refused Christ, it was now too late.

Sometimes, people mock us evangelists for wanting to get people 'saved'. But this is the burden that Jesus himself has placed upon us. As he left the disciples he gave them a command: "Go into all the world and preach the gospel to every creature. He who believes and is baptised will be saved; but he who does not believe will be condemned." (Mark 16:15)

He spoke of the separation of the sheep and goats, the broad and narrow way, the good fish and the bad fish, the wedding banquet, where some were accepted and some were rejected. He spoke of weeping and wailing in outer darkness. Today many people think we are all going to heaven and that hell no longer exists. Just because I say Australia doesn't exist, doesn't stop it existing. Just because you say hell doesn't exist, doesn't stop that existing either. The love of God compels us to call people to receive Jesus Christ who said, "No one comes to the Father except by me." (John 14:6)

Later in that trip, we had a lovely day by Lake Victoria, as I was asked to teach the leadership group from Gaba Community Church. We had a picnic together and a time of singing, fellowship, teaching and laughter. It was a special moment. I felt we could do a lot more trips with very small teams and we agreed to return to Uganda the following year.

In September a team of ten people from Gaba in Uganda visited the UK with drums and traditional dress. When they visited Stowmarket for a week, I took them in schools and to churches and we had great fun sharing the good news. On the Thursday, we brought the market place to a standstill, as they donned their traditional dress and danced to the drums in the middle of the market. Some of them talked to passers-by about Jesus and how they could know him.

I also arranged for them to record a worship tape in the recording studios owned by my good friend, Peter Goodsell. Peter would have loved to have come with me to Africa but was suffering from a serious illness which affected his kidneys and he felt he wouldn't be able to risk the trip. But by the time he had finished two days of recording and mixing the music of the group from Gaba, he felt as if he had been to Uganda for a day. He thoroughly enjoyed it, as did the Ugandans. After this experience, Peter would often give me some money before each African trip to buy him an African drum, so he could build a collection of drums for the percussion workshops he was doing in the UK. I visited a drum workshop near to the equator in Uganda, on one trip, and had my photo taken outside with all the various drums. Peter kept that photo on display in his studio.

None of the Ugandans had ever seen the ocean,

Uganda being landlocked. So, before they left Stowmarket, I took them to the Suffolk coast to the beach at Aldeburgh. We bought them all fish and chips which we ate sitting on the beach – a real English experience.

The group's visit to the UK ended with a concert in Ely Cathedral, called 'African Praise' and organised by Kerry Dixon. The cathedral was packed and Pastor Peter Kasirivu preached a powerful message and prayed for God to visit England again with power.

For the rest of the year life went on as usual. I preached, led services, conducted funerals, spoke on 'thought for the day' on Radio Suffolk, preached to men in Highpoint Prison, took the girls to school and did all the things normal families do. Yet I was very aware that my destiny in God was unfolding before my eyes, even though there were still many hurdles to overcome.

Chapter 18

The woman you put here with me

A letter arrived from the Bishop of Dunwich one morning. I had been negotiating with the diocese about the possibility of phasing out my payments from the diocese, to live by faith but keep the clergy house we were living in. Now this letter had arrived, informing me that from 1 September, the diocese would no longer be paying me and that we would also have to vacate the house. We were facing the loss of income and the house at the same time. It was a huge shock but, with hindsight, it was straight from God's hand. I had been trying to control the situation and smooth the way into what I was trying to do, in a way that required the least amount of faith and trust in God as possible. But this was not God's plan. At the rate I was going, we'd never get there.

I could, of course, have applied for another Church Army job in another parish but that would have been a huge step backwards. At this point, Hazel urged me to 'go for it'. Perhaps too little is written in this book about Hazel's influence. Some people see me as a man of faith, but I can tell you that very little would have been attempted without Hazel's encouragement. Some people have wondered why we don't 'minister together'. I would argue that we do. Hazel isn't a great one for being 'up front' or on the platform. She has instead chosen, with great determination, that while I am here and there – home today, abroad or in another part of the country tomorrow – she will keep the home stable and steady for the children. It has always been so. As a result, she often took the bad news of our son's illness and his eventual death alone, as I was often elsewhere. Nor does she stand at the door and weep as I leave for each trip, though she dislikes me being away.

When God created Eve in the Garden of Eden, he told Adam he was creating a helper 'meet' or suitable for him. Despite our obvious differences, Hazel is a great helper 'suitable' for me and it's hard to see how I could do the ministry without her. Now the children are grown, she has been able to pursue her career and find a great deal of fulfilment in that. She also has the gift of wisdom and often cuts through my ministry problems with an inspired word from God. So when Hazel said 'go for it', I didn't treat it as idle words or immaturity but as a word of authority.

But what was it I was to 'go for'? How did faith work? Where would we live? How would we live? Was I slightly mad? All these questions kept me awake at night.

We began looking at renting a house. Then God impressed upon me that we must buy a house. But how do you buy a house when you are about to lose your job and you have no savings? I began asking God to teach me about faith and how the whole 'faith thing' works. I knew people who said they 'lived by faith' but actually lived on benefits from the State. The deal I struck with God was, I could learn from him about faith but I wasn't going to do the 'living on benefits' thing.

The only thing I knew about faith is that you have to act as though you already have what you need. So we began looking at houses as though we had the means to purchase one. When we eventually found a house, I put in an offer on the day before I went to Africa. But the estate agent said he could only accept the offer if we had a mortgage offer and told him who our solicitor was. I told him I was leaving for Africa the next day at noon.

The following morning I tried to see various mortgage advisors but they were all busy. It was now 11am and I was leaving for Africa in an hour. I went to the estate agent and told him I had failed. He took me up the street and got me an immediate appointment with a friend of his who was a mortgage advisor. I was completely straight with him about our situation. He said there was no problem and he would have several quotes on my return.

Now I needed a solicitor. As we were speaking, a solicitor came into the reception area promoting his new business across the road. I followed him back to his office and signed him up. I got back to the estate agent with minutes to spare. Moments later, I was sitting on a plane leaving for Africa with Adam Waller and my friend Derek Ames. As the huge Jumbo Jet lifted into the air, with no visible means of support, it seemed the perfect symbol of what I had just experienced in buying a house.

Chapter 19

Meeting Rachel

We landed in Entebbe, Uganda and left Derek in the
care of our friend Nathan Amooti for a week, while
Adam and I travelled on to Rwanda. We went by
road, on a crowded public minibus, with our friend
Charles Mugisha, twelve passengers, the driver,
several goats, and a couple of restless chickens. It
was a day-long journey.

At the border, a man in our minibus was arrested,
suspected of carrying messages for the militias
involved in the genocide. We too were interrogated
about our reasons for coming to Rwanda. Eventually,
we left the border, without the unfortunate passenger
who had been arrested, and made our way through
the mountains and tea plantations of Rwanda. I found
it strange to smell tea in the air. The views across
this 'Land of a Thousand Hills' were breathtaking.

The next day we visited a genocide site and I saw
the horror of the killing first-hand, as we went from
room to room in a village school where the bodies
of men, women, and children lay where they had
fallen – skeletons wearing clothes.

It came time for me to preach for the first time in
Rwanda. A very different experience from preaching
anywhere else in Africa. Before I left England, I had
prayed earnestly for God to give me a message for
the people of Rwanda. At one evening service at St

Peter's, in Stowmarket, I had a vision – like a video playing inside my head. I saw a building which was open on three sides and a roof held up by a red steel frame. Hundreds of Rwandans were there and they were all leaning forward, out of their seats with their hands on the ground. When I asked God what this meant, he told me, if a person was sick, we would lay hands on the person and pray for healing. But in Rwanda, that whole land was sick, so I was to tell people to lay hands on the land and pray for its healing. I carried this vision with me to Rwanda.

The following morning in Rwanda I stood at the pulpit in a church in Remera district in Kigali. Over a thousand people had gathered and a local council meeting had been cancelled because most of the members of the committee had come to hear me speak. Few westerners were visiting Rwanda at that time and there was great expectation in the crowd. The pastor introduced me. I stood and looked out at the crowd. Norman Desire, my interpreter, stood by my side, waiting to translate my first sentence. I paused. The words I first read in that Bible, in Mirfield monastery, all those years ago, came flooding back to me.

"A voice was heard in Ramah,
Lamentation, weeping, and great mourning,
Rachel weeping for her children,
Refusing to be comforted,
Because they are no more."
(Matthew 2:18)

Now I stood, looking into the eyes of Rachel – many Rachels.

"Can Rwanda be healed?" I began. A divine authority hung in the air.

"Ese u Rwanda rushobora gukira?" Norman repeated in translation.

"Can Rwanda be healed?" I repeated.

"Ese u Rwanda rushobora gukira?" Norman echoed.

I told the story of my parents and our son dying, and how God had brought us through that terrible experience. Women wept openly as I told the story. I was surprised because their stories were so much worse than mine. But that day, as the tears of many Rachels fell to the dusty ground, somehow I became one with the people of Rwanda. In grief. In hope. In Christ.

As I ended my message, about fifty people received Jesus into their hearts. The people were so hungry, so dry – thirsting for hope. I told them to put their hand on their head. I prayed that God would take away the nightmares. I told them to put their hand on their heart. I prayed God would heal broken hearts and give them a new heart as he promised in Ezekiel 36:26. Finally, I told them to put their hands on the ground and we prayed for the land of Rwanda to be healed of bloodshed. It was a moment of divine visitation. Many small pools of tears remained on the dusty floor as we left. "Rachel weeping for her children because they are no more."

After the meeting darkness fell. Adam and I were taken to the home of my friend Phocas Ngendahayo. We had some food with people from the church. They told us their stories. All of them had lost family members in the genocide. As we stood to leave, a lady called Agnes took my hand. She introduced her daughters and told me how her husband and sons had been murdered in the genocide. She looked deep into my eyes and said, "Thank you. Because you have come to us, we know that God has not forgotten us." I felt a lump in my throat. We walked back through the dark African night, to the convent where we were staying, accompanied only by the sound of crickets.

The next day, Monday, I was asked to speak at a lunch-hour meeting in the centre of Kigali. In England, a lunch-hour meeting is going well if we get twenty people. So I was slightly shocked to arrive to a crowd of over 1,200 people. More surprising, as I sat on the stage waiting to speak, was the venue. It seemed familiar. It was open on three sides and had a roof held up by a red steel frame... Yes. This was the building I had seen in the vision back in England as I had asked God to give me a vision for Rwanda. This was an appointment with destiny.

I preached about the blood of Abel crying from the ground. I asked the question, if God was disturbed by the blood of one man – and his blood could be heard in heaven, crying from the ground – what must the sound of the blood of one million Rwandans sound like to God?

Cain asked God, "Am I my brother's keeper?" God didn't answer, but the rest of the Bible gives a resounding "Yes!" We are our brother's keeper. We are to look after each other. We are responsible.

As all 1,200 people laid hands on the ground and prayed for their land to be healed, I knew that God had brought me here for a purpose. Again, many women wept bitterly for their dead children. Rachel weeping...

Later in the week we held a four-day conference at the church in Remera. Charles was eager that we pray for the sick. So, on the last day we offered prayer for the sick. Many people came forward for ministry. We began to pray. We prayed and we prayed like never before. It seemed like there was an anointing for breakthrough. Suddenly there was a commotion in the crowd. A lady was calling out. Norman was speaking to her but it was all in Kinyarwanda so I couldn't understand.

Eventually, Norman turned to me and said, "She is saying she has been here the past few days listening to you preaching. But she didn't know you were a mzungu (white man) because she has been blind for twelve years. As we were praying, her eyes opened and she can see your white face and the faces of her friends."

A young woman came forward who had also been blind. She told the crowd how her eyes had been opened as we prayed.

Another lady climbed onto the platform and began touching her toes. She told us how she had constant severe abdominal pain but now she was healed as we prayed – she touched her toes to prove it. A string of healing testimonies ensued.

Once you have experienced that miracle atmosphere, you know that God can do anything at any time and you expect things to happen. I knew we would be returning to Rwanda.

Chapter 20

Up a mountain without a paddle

Mount Elgon sits on the border of Kenya and Uganda, several miles from the Ugandan town of Mbale. Derek Ames, one of our trustees, had been corresponding with a young man from one of the villages near the mountain summit. We had been invited to lead a mission to the area by Arphaxad, the Archdeacon of the area.

Adam and I had just come from the two-week mission in Rwanda and I was tired. But before we returned home, we had to do another week of mission in this remote area of Uganda. It was miles from civilisation or a tarmac road. I would be preaching every day for a week. Halfway through this mission, I was really longing to go home. The people of that village gave us the very best of everything they had. They didn't have much but what they had they gave. We stayed in the only house for probably a hundred miles that had a flush toilet. I was so thankful for that.

However, we were cooking for ourselves. There were three of us and a camping stove. So catering was not our strong point. The beds had bedbugs and we were being bitten every night while we tried to sleep. We also had a full day's journey, along muddy roads, to get back to the city before we left for home.

We had built a platform at the edge of the village football field and about one thousand people gathered every night to hear the preaching. I retold the stories of Jesus' parables as the culture they related to was so similar to the village life there. They kept sheep and goats. They sowed seed and reaped a harvest. They had sons and daughters. They had weddings. Every night around a hundred people received Jesus into their heart. As we prayed for the sick most of the crowd pressed towards the platform. On the last night, several hardened teenagers came and repented and received Christ, to great cheers from the whole village.

On the last night, I told the Archdeacon we were working with, that we would have to leave early in the morning. He wanted a meeting in the morning but I knew that would lead to long repetitive speeches of thanks that, as far as I was concerned were totally unnecessary. I tried to put him off so we could get away early.

During the night there was torrential rain. The bus couldn't reach our house at the top of a muddy hill. So we had to carry all our belongings for half a mile, walking through thick mud with our suitcases on our head. We arrived at the bottom of the hill looking like refugees from a war. Our shoes were covered with thick mud and our trousers had muddy wet stains up to our knees.

Then I got a message that the Archdeacon had arranged a communion service at the church and was waiting for us. The church was another half-mile walk in thick mud. I'm afraid I 'lost it'. I totally refused to walk to the church for a communion service. A messenger was sent to tell the Archdeacon I was not coming. A message came back that, 'the Lord's table is set and the Archdeacon is waiting'. I reasoned with myself that it would obviously upset this man if I didn't go but on the other hand, after today, I would never see him again. So I stubbornly refused to go. I felt bad, as in the end one of my team went on my behalf, so I still had to wait to go home.

As we left, the driver wanted to take a short cut but the bridge over the river was down. After a lot of arguing they decided to drive the bus through the river, at a point where four-wheel drive vehicles had been crossing. Needless to say, the bus was too long and got jammed – the front and rear ends stuck on opposite banks of the small river. Things were just getting worse. After more than an hour of digging, pushing, praying and a little help from a man with a tractor, the bus was finally freed. We left for the long journey back to Kampala. As we arrived home in the UK, I felt I had not done the right thing in refusing to meet the Archdeacon but was sure I'd never meet him again.

Six months later, the Archdeacon was given a grant to visit the UK. Inevitably, after he arrived in the UK and made a few phone calls, he was sitting in my front room and I was eating humble pie with a large spoon. Fortunately for me, he was very gracious. For the cost of a bit of grace and patience

– and an hour or two of my time – I could have done the right thing. The world is a small place and we are probably going to meet people again, however fleeting our original meeting. What did I learn from this? Don't burn your bridges. As far as it depends on you, do the right thing – even if the right thing is also the hard thing to do.

Shortly after the mission, I found myself in Torquay on the J. John retreat. I knew John, Andy Economides and a few others there had gone before me – stepping out in faith to establish an independently financed ministry. I chatted to several of the guys to ask how they went about it. Over drinks one evening, I said to J. John, "How do I get from where I am, to where you are?" I wasn't talking about his success or fame but his freedom to minister and follow his calling.

"Mate, just buy a house and go for it!" was his profound reply.

Actually, as I look back over the last eight years, I now believe that is exactly what you have to do. What sounded initially like a glib reply was actually the voice of great experience and wisdom. In order to pioneer anything, that really is the best advice. Just go for it! If God is calling you, he who gives the vision will also give the provision. If God is calling you, "Mate, just buy a house and go for it!"

Back in Stowmarket we had announced our decision to stay in the area and live by faith. To be honest, I don't think any of the trustees were brimming over with faith. Quite the opposite. But shortly before we came to take the step of faith we had announced, a couple asked to speak to me at church. They knew nothing of our situation, having been absent when it was announced. After the service one morning, they gave me a cheque for the Trust for £6,500. That was more than the Trust received in the whole of the previous year. Call me naive but I took that as an encouragement from God that he would supply, not only all the needs of the Trust, but all our personal needs as well.

Wendy Diaper, one of our trustees at the time, received a word from the Lord about the Trust finances. As she was reading her Bible, she came across these words which she felt were about the finances of the ministry.

> "This year you will eat what grows by itself,
> and the second year what springs from that.
> But in the third year sow and reap, plant
> vineyards and eat their fruit."
>   (Isaiah 37:30)

It seemed odd to read that at the time but with the benefit of hindsight it came to be true. The finances did seem to just grow by themselves the first year. Support in the second year sprang from what we did in the first year. Then there was a warning, "But in the third year sow and reap, plant vineyards and eat their fruit." I wasn't sure what this meant at the time.

St Peter's then decided they would support the Trust by tithing their income to the Trust for three years. This they faithfully did. God's warning did indicate that we needed to act in the third year as our income sources would change.

At the end of two years, I met with Charles Mugisha in London. We often meet in a cafe in Liverpool Street Station. It is a useful place to hold meetings with people from the South or Africans who are staying in London. There is a fast train to Liverpool Street from Stowmarket so I can get there and back comfortably in a day.

As we met in the cafe that day, I was wondering in my heart what form these 'vineyards' would take. Charles was carrying in his heart a burden to start a child sponsorship programme in Rwanda. He believed education was the key to Rwanda's future. I wasn't sure if we wanted something that would generate that level of administration but I had told Charles to get me the details of five children and we could see how it went. He arrived at the cafe with the details of eleven children. "They are all friends!" he explained. "I couldn't give some hope and not the others."

I took the papers and looked through the photos of the children. We talked at length about how it would work. Charles had worked for Compassion International for many years as a local coordinator for child sponsorship in Uganda. So he seemed an expert in how it all worked, both in Africa and at the donor end. As I write, we have about three hundred children sponsored through the ministry and the system is pretty much the same system we set up that day in the cafe.

Since that day we have planted many 'vineyards'. They are places of growth and help for the poor. As I have been faithful in planting the vineyards to help the poor, God has been faithful in supplying, not only the needs of those projects, but all the needs and more of the Trust in the UK and elsewhere. We are just completing the building of an orphanage – The House of Mercy. We feed two hundred street children twice a week. And we do so much more because God is faithful.

Hazel and I received an official farewell from St Peter's in Stowmarket at a Communion service on 2 August 1998. As we sang the final hymn, Hazel passed me a Bible and pointed to a verse.

"I think this is from God," she said. The verse read:

> "See, today I am freeing you from the chains on your wrists. Come with me to Babylon, if you like, and I will look after you; but if you do not want to, then don't come. Look, the whole country lies before you; go wherever you please."
>
> (Jeremiah 40:4)

It could have been written personally to me. I had felt chained to the parish ministry and longed for freedom. I had taken the steps of praying, setting up the Trust and talking about the vision to everyone I met. Now God had spoken. He had freed me from the chains on my wrists. My hands were free to work the purpose for which I was made. As I read the words I was moved to tears.

There were kind words of appreciation and support in the service. There was a parish barbecue at the vicarage where everyone came to say farewell. It was also the anniversary of Philip's birth. But the one thing that moved me most that day was the word from God that I was at last free. To quote Martin Luther King, "Free at last. Free at last. Thank God almighty, we are free at last!"

Chapter 21

The Danish pastry and the alarmed nuns

It's amazing how much junk you acquire when you have space. As Hazel and I tried to scale down our life from a large and spacious four bedroom detached house, to a small three bedroom semi (without a garage!) we realised it wasn't all going to fit. We had been ruthless in getting rid of so much stuff but one thing was obvious – there was no room for the ministry office in our new house. However, I limped along, squashed into a corner, first in the bedroom and then in the dining room. Eventually, I got faith that we could rent an office in town. It took another breakthrough but it was one of the best things we ever did, when we moved the office out of the house into separate office premises.

As 1999 unfolded we held another mission to Rwanda with a few days in Uganda. Joining me on the team that year was Catharine Morris, who had been a little girl during our Holy Family days but had just been accepted for ordination training. Mike Smith, a local pastor from Stowmarket, who was also a trustee, joined the team. And finally, my good friend Hil Jennings, a piano tuner.

In Rwanda we worked with Charles and also our old friend Nathan Amooti. Nathan had also moved back from Uganda to his homeland of Rwanda. At the invitation of the Archbishop of Rwanda he had been ordained as an Anglican priest and appointed as a development officer, working from the cathedral offices. Nathan had arranged a mission for us in the town of Nyamata. The idea was to hold a clergy conference for about one hundred clergy and then follow that with an evangelistic outreach into the town.

However, when we arrived on the first day, over a thousand people were waiting for us. We had a brief meeting with the clergy to introduce ourselves. We agreed that some of these people had walked over thirty miles to get there. We couldn't keep them waiting for days while we had a clergy conference behind closed doors. But there were too many of them for the church building. We agreed to start the meetings in the open air outside the church. So began a week-long conference. Our interpreter for this conference was Canon Peter, one of the clergy from Kigali. As the week unfolded I called for people to receive Jesus into their heart and then we prayed for the sick. After two days, I felt God prompting me to ask if anyone had been healed. I really didn't want to do it. I wrestled with my reluctance. In the end I was obedient and asked the crowd on Wednesday morning if anyone had been healed during the meetings. About two-thirds of the people raised their hands. I asked them to tell their stories. Over and over people testified to being healed as I had prayed for the sick on the first night.

A man at the side of the crowd began dancing – hopping from one leg to the other. I asked Canon

Peter what he was saying.

"He is saying," Canon Peter replied, "that four men carried him to the meeting because he was crippled in both legs. But as you prayed on the first night, his legs were healed. He is dancing to show the crowd he is really healed!"

On Thursday I preached about receiving the living water of the Holy Spirit. At the end of my message the whole crowd stood as we asked God to baptise everyone with the Holy Spirit. Everyone began to call on God at the same time. The sound was like the sound of many waters. Someone thought a helicopter passed overhead. Others said it thundered. What I remember is that the presence of God came down in power that day. In that place, that was so touched by the East African Revival years earlier, we felt and heard the presence of the Living God. By the end of the week, hundreds had given their lives to Christ and many more had been healed by God. Everyone had been encouraged.

"The money just came in!" It was my friend Andy Ellis. We had been planning to go on a mission to Tanzania. I had been contacted earlier in the year by Captain Ray Mills of the Church Army. A friend of his from Nairobi in Kenya had invited him to preach in a mission to refugees in Tanzania. François Nitunga was from Burundi but lived in Kenya as a refugee from the war in his homeland. He had invited Ray Mills to share in his mission but Ray had told him, "I don't do crusades in Africa but I know a man who does." Ray had passed my details to François. At the time, things were financially tight in the ministry and we didn't seem to have enough money to go to Tanzania. But we explored some dates with François. Andy Ellis had been speaking about coming with me on an African trip and so we planned to go together. At the time, Andy was looking for work, so financially the trip seemed in doubt. Miraculously, the money came in for both of us. I emailed François with the news. He arranged for us to meet him in Nairobi and then fly to Tanzania the following day.

As Andy and I emerged into the arrivals lobby in Jomo Kenyata airport in Nairobi, we met François for the first time. Until now we had only communicated through email and the odd phone call. François took us to Mayfield, a guest-house owned by Africa Inland Mission (AIM). It was run by Americans and people of many nationalities were staying there. The rooms were pleasant enough.

François explained that he had booked Andy and me on the flight the following day but there was no room for him so he would follow and meet us the day after. This disturbed me because it meant we would be venturing into a new country alone, unable to speak the language. François told us he had arranged for someone to meet us at Mwanza, the halfway point. He would meet us there and fly the rest of the way with us. It was only because François was a member of Church Army that I felt able to agree with this arrangement but it left me a little uneasy.

Next morning we arrived at Wilson Domestic Airport and discovered that some people had cancelled. François was still not able to come as he hadn't brought his things. We walked across the tarmac to find a little six-seater aircraft waiting for us. The flight was with Mission Aviation Fellowship. It was to be just Andy and me with the pilot. I had never been in such a small aircraft before. I was slightly unnerved as the pilot explained how to open the door in the event of a crash in which he didn't survive. The aircraft felt a bit flimsy as it rattled down the runway and droned into the air. It was a clear sunny day and there were breathtaking views of Kilimanjaro on the horizon which took our mind off things, as the slums of Nairobi slipped away below us.

After an hour or two we descended into Mwanza airport where dozens of small aircraft were resting from their travels. We were now at our first stop in Tanzania and didn't know any of the local language. Amazingly, after a lot of people shouted things at us, we cleared immigration. A lady met us in the foyer who communicated that she was a friend of François. We showed her the scrap of paper François had written his recommended guest-house on. "Yes," she said. She asked a few strange questions but whatever question we asked she just said, "Yes".

"What time is it here?" we asked.

"Yes," she said.

"What time will François come tomorrow?"

"Yes," she replied.

We checked into the guest-house where we shared a room with two cockroaches and a mosquito. Under the window, in the shade of a large tree, the local men discussed the issues of the day with the shoeshine man. Andy and I went for a walk as the sun set over Lake Victoria. The East Africa railway ran through the town and an old British-built diesel shunter rattled past us. As we walked by the lake we were were taken by the beauty of the place. Women and children ran to sell us bananas and mangoes. We walked back into the town to try and find somewhere to eat – the dining room at the guest-house looked grim. Above a shop on the main street we found a place advertising "Chips and English food". The menu was limited. We tried to order omelette and chips as we thought you couldn't really make a mess of that. "You want chips with your omelette or separate?" The waiter asked in broken English.

It seemed a strange question. When we said we'd like our chips with the omelette he seemed very surprised. We wondered why you would want them separate?

Two large omelettes arrived. "Where are the chips?" we asked.

"They are 'with' the omelette," the waiter replied.

For 'with' read 'in'! They had cooked the chips in the omelette. It was unusual but edible.

We returned to the guest-house and were shown

to the toilet by a helpful cockroach. We settled in the room and under our mosquito nets as darkness fell. There was a lot of shouting around the shoeshine stall but eventually we drifted into a fitful sleep.

In the morning, we were met by François and caught another six-seater Cessna from Mwanza to Kageera. After droning above the mountains of the Kagera region of Tanzania and Rwanda for a couple of hours, I noticed that the pilot was descending. I was a bit disturbed by this as all I could see below were the mountains – no sign of a town or city anywhere. Still the plane descended. There in the distance I saw a small line on the ground. It was a short dirt landing-strip. No tarmac and certainly no airport.

As we touched down, I saw a soldier with a gun sitting by a mud hut at the end of the landing-strip. The plane jerked to a halt and the pilot switched off the engine. While we retrieved our luggage from the plane, Canon Anania Nkware arrived to welcome us. Our bags were loaded into a four-wheel drive as we talked. I heard the plane engine fire up and then watched the plane buzz down the runway and take off into the distance.

"It comes every Wednesday" the Canon told me.

Oh dear, I thought. We are in the middle of nowhere and whatever happens, there is no way home until next Wednesday at the earliest. I had not really appreciated how remote this place would be. The Canon, as he was known, had been the vicar of a quiet rural parish in this corner of Tanzania until 100,000 refugees poured over the border to escape the genocide and subsequent war in neighbouring Rwanda. The press and many aid agencies had long gone but 20,000 displaced people remained in refugee camps. They were from Burundi and Rwanda – all fleeing their homeland in fear of being killed. Some had fled then returned, only to flee a second time when fighting flared up again in their own countries.

As we drove to our accommodation, the most striking thing was that the land had been stripped of trees. This was once home to Tanzania's giraffe population but now the animals had left to look for food in a less-populated area. The stripping of trees for firewood was beginning to cause serious soil erosion in this mountain region.

We arrived at our home for the next two weeks. It had originally been a feeding centre for the refugees, run by Danish aid workers. Some of the buildings were just containers with windows cut into them. Andy and I were shown to a small hut on one side of a quadrangle of makeshift buildings. A group of African ladies ran this impromptu guest-house when visitors came. Each day they looked after us, cooking our meals and making tea and coffee. The bathroom facilities were in two places. There was an open-air shower across the yard from our room. A cubicle of corrugated iron sheets, topped with an old oil drum which collected rainwater from the roof, made up the shower. As the sun went down I stood under the shower's cold flow and looked up to watch a flock of birds flying majestically across a breathtaking sunset. Showering in the open air was quite different from home.

"The Danish people taught us to make cakes," the ladies told us. "Would you like us to make some for you?"

I politely accepted but was unsure what sort of baking would arrive – these ladies only had an open fire to cook on. How do you make edible cakes over a few burning logs?

Incredibly, the ladies arrived a couple of hours later, with pots of tea and perfect Danish pastries in the tin hut dining room. The pastries looked like they had just been purchased from our local bakery. Thank God for the Danish group who had lived here during the worst years of the displacement.

The toilet facilities were set apart from the other buildings. The word 'facilities' is perhaps misleading. There was a corrugated iron sheet hut about six feet square which housed nothing more than a small hole in the ground. A small black and white lizard lurked in the corner catching insects with his tongue. As I went to sleep in our little hut that night, I asked myself the question I have asked so many times, "Lord, what on earth am I doing here?"

As the days unfolded I spent my time speaking to clergy, pastors and community leaders from the refugees. Every afternoon at four I preached at a crusade in the camp. About two thousand refugees attended each afternoon. I called people to receive Jesus as their Saviour and we prayed for the sick. Many became Christians and many people testified to being healed by Jesus as we prayed. When I asked one lady what Jesus had done for her she said, "I was blind but now I can see."

François and the other clergy were totally committed to these poor people and I grew in my admiration for their work. When Andy and I returned to England the Canon sent me a moving letter of appreciation.

Rusumo Parish, Ngara, Tanzania.

Dear Brother Don,

Greetings in the name of our Lord Jesus Christ. I would like to take this opportunity to thank you for the blessings you left with us during the September Mission in the Refugee Camp.

I have been receiving many testimonies from people who got healed from different diseases, e.g. my daughter who recovered her sight, my sister who had had a heart attack, one man and woman who were suffering for so many years with T.B. and were ready to die. Many in the camp got healed and continue giving their testimonies concerning the healing power of Jesus Christ.

Revd Canon Aninia Nkware.

One of the reasons I wrote this book is that strange things happen to me. Not least of these was when the Northern Anglo Catholic Charismatic Convention asked me to speak at their annual conference. Some of the committee knew me from my days at Holy Family in Manchester where I became a Christian. The conference was held in a convent in Belper, Derbyshire. A group of ageing nuns lived in community and ran the conference centre. Their days seemed numbered as the community was in decline and advanced in years. The finances were difficult too. Some of the sisters were bedridden.

On the first night of the conference I was shown to my room. A typical convent bedroom with simple furnishings. On the window-sill in the corridor, just outside my room, I noticed four tins of fly spray and thought that was a little curious. However, as I turned in for the night I found out the reason they were there.

In the darkness I heard the annoying buzz of a bluebottle. I put the light on and thought I'd swat the blighter so I could sleep. I chased it around the room and managed to swat it. I put the light off and returned to bed. To my annoyance I then heard two flies. I put the light back on. My previous prey lay dead on the floor but there were, indeed, two new flies buzzing around the light. I managed to bring them both down after moving around the room like a martial arts expert, magazine in hand.

The situation repeated itself and each time the number of insects doubled. New weapons had to be found and I went into the corridor to arm myself with one of the tins of fly spray. I covered my mouth with a handkerchief and sprayed the poison into the air. One by one the enemy fell to the ground.

Yet every time I put the light out, reinforcements seemed to appear from nowhere. I located the source as the light fitting on the ceiling. The battle raged for what seemed like hours. I had never seen so many flies in one place. Eventually, there was just one left. I was now standing on the bed with a can of spray in each hand, fully alert and ready for the next attack. It seemed there was just one insect left alive – the corpses of all the rest covered the floor. The target landed on the smoke detector on the ceiling. I approached quietly and released a small blast from the fly spray. Immediately, the fire alarm sounded. It was one of those moments when you wish you could just rewind time and not do what you just did. Of course, the spray had set off the fire alarm.

I thought of all the bed-ridden nuns about to be evacuated because of my error. I got dressed and ran down the corridor to find Keith Ashworth, the chairman of the conference, looking dazed and wondering what to do.

"It's a false alarm!" I called, wondering how to explain the story of the plague of flies. Eventually the alarm was reset and the sisters were assured all would be well. I don't think my story was believed as I had a lecture the following morning from one of the sisters.

"You mustn't smoke in your room, dear!" she told me.

"No, I don't smoke." I told her as I tried to communicate the events of the previous evening.

"You can smoke outside but not in your room. You should have read the signs we've put up," she said.

But I don't smoke! I thought. Even when I showed her all the corpses of the culprits she still didn't believe me. I imagined the headlines in the local press – "Evangelist alarms Nuns!"

Chapter 22

Difficult times

More than enough has been said and written about the period when Trevor Jones was vicar of St Peter's Stowmarket. I don't want to add to that but, for the purpose of understanding this story, I include a brief report from the Daily Telegraph dated 27 October 2000.

Vicar faces jail again after admitting fraud

By Victoria Combe, Religion Correspondent

A VICAR with a criminal record stretching back to the Sixties is facing his second jail sentence after he admitted fraud charges yesterday.

The Revd Trevor Jones, vicar of St Peter and St Mary, Stowmarket, Suffolk, had toured prisons since 1992 preaching to inmates about how he had found God and turned his back on crime.

But at Ipswich Crown Court this week, he was accused of swindling his parish out of £26,663, including £1,000 collected for the needy, to pay his own debts. Jones changed his plea yesterday, three days into his trial, and admitted four of 12 charges of dishonesty.

Jones, 50, pleaded guilty to charges of false

accounting, of obtaining services by deception and of obtaining a money transfer by deception. The remaining eight charges were ordered to lie on file and the case adjourned until Nov 20.

Outside court, Jones burst into tears, saying: "It's the saddest day of my life. When you look at this, it seems I have come full circle. Being back here today seems very ironic."

Before he became a priest, Jones had various jobs including oil rig worker and builder. He committed his first offence of dishonesty in 1967 and two years later was sent to borstal for driving offences. He received an 18-month sentence for conspiracy to burgle in 1970.

In June 1983, he was jailed for six months with another 12 months suspended at Norwich Crown Court after he admitted eight offences of deception involving building work and asked for another 53 offences to be considered.

Jones said outside court: "Sorry is a very bland term. It covers a lot of stuff. It is very difficult when you look at this. It looks dishonest. Stupid. You plead guilty to something because it is true. There has been a great deal of stupidity, foolishness and at the end of this it is what I will be remembered for."

Needless to say that what appeared in the press as a couple of days in court, had huge repercussions over several years for the congregation involved.

Chapter 23

The man who gave his shoes away

The years following Trevor's arrest were wilderness years for Hazel and me. We didn't seem to fit in church. We tried a few churches and we tried worshipping separately at different churches but nothing seemed right. This unsatisfactory situation lasted for the next few years. But we had to press on and live life through the wilderness.

My Greek friend Andy Economides invited me to join him on a trip to Nigeria, along with Ian Wilson, a dentist and evangelist, and ex-footballer Mick Mellows. Andy's ministry, Soteria Trust, has a great work in Nigeria, sponsoring children's education, giving scholarships and building a school in Ibadan. Alongside these activities, Andy also conducts large-scale crusades once or twice a year.

Up until this point, I only had experience of East Africa. Nigeria is a completely different culture and I had to tune in again to learn the workings of a new culture. The first notable difference was the large number of Mercedes on the roads. This was an African country with money, certainly in the hands of a few. As we drove from the airport into Lagos, one did see all the usual African poverty. Mile after mile of slums with rusty corrugated iron sheet roofs. Children stood at traffic lights with a handful of dead rats to prove the traps they were selling worked. The road was marked with three lanes but there seemed to be five or six lanes of traffic all competing for road space.

We turned into the forecourt of the Sheraton Hotel in Lagos. Andy checked us in and we were shown to our rooms. I had always run missions on the basis that we would stay in the cheapest accommodation, so this was new territory for me. It was so good after seven hours on a long-haul flight, in an economy class seat, to have a proper room with a proper bathroom. I stood under a hot shower and thanked God for the privilege of being invited on this trip as a guest of Soteria Trust.

We had a very pleasant meal together with Samuel Folohan, our Nigerian host, and then sat and talked for a while before we turned in for sleep.

Next morning, we left for the city of Ibadan several hours drive away. We checked in at the Premier Hotel, much more downmarket from the Lagos Sheraton, but more than adequate for our needs.

Then began a week of mission when we visited Prospect College and met the students sponsored by Soteria Trust. We visited the school building project. I was greatly moved by the school and began wondering if we could do something similar in Rwanda. It was such an inspiration. Andy's situation was in some ways similar to mine in that he had worked for the Anglican Church for some years before founding his own Trust to develop his ministry as an evangelist. So this was all a great learning experience about what could be achieved.

In the evenings we took part in a crusade held at the church. Thousands of people packed the building which was like an aircraft hangar and open on all sides. The building overflowed. Andy preached passionately, as he always does, about our need to receive Jesus Christ into our heart.

Hundreds of people responded to his message and ran forward to give their hearts to Jesus. After Andy had prayed with them he told the people we would pray for the sick. He then asked me to take over and lead the healing part of the meeting. I was quite moved by the trust this man placed in me.

About one thousand people came forward for healing and the four of us men waded through the crowds to lay hands on the sick who now surrounded the platform. Cries and shrieks went up from the crowd as the power of God moved among them.

Thousands of voices were lifted up in prayer at the same time. It was like the sound of many waters. On and on they prayed. Women were weeping. Men shook. Some fell under the power. A lady lifted her baby above the crowd that we might touch him. On and on it went, the noise rising to a crescendo and then, after many minutes, it became quiet with only the sound of sobbing to be heard here and there. Still we ministered, touching the sick and desperately poor.

Andy pulled a man from the crowd who was barefoot. He took off his own shoes and gave them to the man. These were Andy's best shoes. This is typical of the man. I have seen him do similar things many times. What an inspiration.

As the meeting closed we helped Andy across the muddy road, in his socks, to the car and back to the hotel. The night had been a great adventure. Hundreds had met with Jesus. Many had been healed and touched by the power of God. A poor man had been given an expensive pair of shoes. Touching heaven. Changing earth.

The mission was one of the best I have been on in Africa. It was also a great joy to get to know Mick Mellows as we shared a room and also to get to know Ian Wilson better.

Ian is a dentist and also an evangelist. In the middle of this mission, we helped Ian run a dental clinic for the poor. We ran one clinic upstairs in an old building. A few of the assembled patients were allowed in and sat on a long wooden bench. Ian identified those needing extractions and then went down the line giving an anaesthetic injection to each one. As he did, there was a power cut and the room went black. Someone passed me a torch and I became Ian's assistant shining the light into each mouth as the teeth were extracted.

The only other light was the glow from the gas stove where the instruments were being sterilised. The ten people on the bench were sent to recuperate in the corner until the bleeding stopped and the next ten people were brought in and the process repeated many times. I remember Andy Economides walking up and down the room shaking his head and saying,

"This is amazing! This is amazing!" And he was right. It was amazing. Hundreds of the poor, who would never be able to afford dentistry were relieved of chronic tooth pain as problems were dealt with. It was an amazing mission.

Our last two nights were spent back at the Sheraton Hotel in Lagos. After ministering in a large church in Lagos we had a day to unwind. Overseas missions are always exhausting and it used to take me three weeks to get over one. But I learned something from Andy on this trip. A day to pause, reflect, refresh and relax before travelling back home is very wise. We landed back in the UK early in the morning and by two o'clock that afternoon I was back in the office catching up with work. It was such a dramatic lesson, I vowed I would never do missions the old way again. I would plan a 'sabbath rest' into each mission with space to relax, refresh and restore myself before returning home. That decision transformed the way I do ministry.

A few months later I joined Andy again on a mission to Jersey along with comedian John Archer. Andy was working with a group of churches in Jersey who had organised a series of dinners where John would perform and Andy or I would speak.

I stayed with a couple from one of the churches along with John Archer. We shared a guest room. I thought I'd best warn John that I snored. "Not as much as me!" John replied. He was right!

It was great to work with John and see people respond to his comedy routine. The three of us went into Jersey's prison over a couple of days and met with a group of men there. The first day was hard going but the second day there seemed to be a breakthrough among the men as some asked Jesus into their lives.

One day I spoke at a lunch for business men and then went to speak to a small congregation from the Portuguese church. There are quite a number of Portuguese on Jersey who tend to come to do manual labour on the island. So there is an identifiable community with their own language, culture and church. It was strange preaching so close to home through an interpreter.

That same year I received a letter from Lambeth Palace inviting me to apply for membership of the Archbishops' College of Evangelists. This is not an educational establishment but a group of evangelists recognised and approved by the Archbishops of Canterbury and York. After an interview at Church House in Westminster and the approval of my Diocesan Bishop, at the end of October, Hazel and I travelled to York where, along with a few others, I was enrolled by the Archbishop of York into the College of Evangelists. It doesn't amount to much really, but it is good to have some recognition from the church occasionally.

Chapter 24

Miriam's car and the vineyard

Charles and I were sitting in my office in Stowmarket as Charles shared his vision to build a school in Rwanda. I had been very moved and inspired by the school Soteria Trust had built in Nigeria, but right now we had no money. I was in the middle of telling Charles that I loved the vision but we had no money, when the phone rang. It was my friend Miriam Smith, who had given me the word to 'Go into all the world and preach the gospel', in 1993.

"Is Charles with you?" she demanded.

"Yes," I replied.

"Can you come round and see me straight away and bring Charles with you?" she asked.

Anyone else I would have refused but I knew Miriam would have a good reason to make such a demand, so we went straight away to Miriam's house. As we went I continued to tell Charles we didn't really have the financial capacity to get involved in the building of a school. When we arrived at Miriam's house, she made some coffee and then sat down with us like a president about to discuss an international treaty. A stack of twenty pound notes lay on the table.

"Now," began Miriam, "my eyesight has got very poor and they won't let me drive any more.

So I've sold my car for one thousand pounds. This is the money," she said, pointing, to the cash on the table.

"Now, I don't really need this money. I've got a home, food to eat and clothes to wear. So I want to give this money to you, Don, but I want you to use it to help children in Rwanda."

I looked at Charles as a smile spread across his face. He didn't want to miss the opportunity.

"Thank you," he said. "This money could be used to buy a piece of land to build a school." It really seemed to me that this was God's way of contradicting me – we did have enough financial capacity to help build the school but it would be by faith not by sight.

That was on a Monday. On Wednesday of the same week, I told a friend the story of what happened. He was so impressed he gave me five hundred pounds toward the school.

Charles and I later met in London and discussed starting a child sponsorship programme to cover the costs of children's education and medical care. I was very aware that such a scheme would generate much more administration and at that time I had no administrative help. I suggested Charles register a few children and we could see how it went.

When Charles got back to Rwanda, he found a suitable piece of land for a school building but the price was two thousand pounds. Faith was rising so we added five hundred pounds from general funds and sent the full amount. We also sent four hundred pounds for an architect's plan for the school.

Charles sent me the details of eleven children and we soon found sponsors for all of them. We registered more children and soon had a scheme helping fifty children with their education. As we shared the vision of the school, people began to give so we could start building. Then, out of the blue, I got a call from Charles to say he was going to America for three years to study for his Masters degree. I asked him to think about it as I could see no way the work in Rwanda could continue without him. He was the key person. He told me that he was actually leaving in two weeks' time.

I really felt the work in Rwanda would now be on hold until his return. The other thing that crossed my mind was, what if Charles went to live in America and liked it so much he never came back?

However, I need not have worried. I began emailing his young brother Fred after Charles left for the States. Fred was appointed with executive powers to act on Charles' behalf. I had known Fred as the young youth pastor leading the youth of the church out there. Somehow, Fred just rose to the challenge and proved what a great organiser he was. The child sponsorship scheme continued to grow under his management and the foundations for the school were put in. The school building had many setbacks but the pressure was on as Fred and Charles had started to rent a small house in which they started a school. Children were coming from everywhere to get an education. Everyone wanted to be sponsored for school. Throughout this period, Miriam often rang and asked me to call round. Once she had saved up for a new stereo system but when she got the money she decided instead to give it to the school building project.

"We need to get this school built," she kept telling me.

The following year we had contributed over eight thousand pounds towards the school. Fred and also Charles had recruited support from other sources and soon the first seven classrooms were built along with three offices. The school opened with three hundred and sixty children on the first day of term.

Miriam, now in her eighties, was suddenly taken ill with brain cancer and rushed to hospital just before Christmas. I received a picture by email of all the children queuing to get in the school on the first day. I printed it out and took it with me when I visited Miriam in hospital. We chatted about her illness and then she asked me about the school in Rwanda. I showed her the picture of all the children waiting to get into the school. A tear came to her eye.

"That's marvellous, isn't it?" she said.

She looked at the photo and said, "Perhaps my work is done now."

We prayed together at her bedside. Two days later she died.

I was away when Miriam's funeral took place

but sent a message which was read out by the man who conducted the funeral.

"I know Miriam was ready for heaven. The question is, is heaven ready for Miriam?"

When I first set up the ministry as a registered charity I hadn't foreseen that we would begin to relieve poverty to this extent. The relief of poverty was not one of our objectives in the trust deed. Unfortunately, for legal reasons the deed could not be changed. So we began the process of registering another charity which we called 'The RSVP Trust'. We had already adopted RSVP as a working name because nobody could remember, spell or pronounce 'The Evangelism Fellowship'. God has invited us all to a party that is out of this world. But we need to RSVP the invitation. So that was the name we settled on for the new charity. In reality, I had felt after the RSVP '93 mission in Stowmarket, that God told me to set up a ministry called RSVP. But sometimes we just don't catch what God is saying until a bit later, do we?

Chapter 25

The Massai and the missing suitcase

David Kereto visited our office in Stowmarket. David was a Massai. He was over in the UK for a conference and had found our details in a directory of Christian ministries. He came to see me to talk about the possibility of doing a mission among the Massai people in Narok, Kenya. I told him we would pray about it. We kept in touch by email and the following year we planned a week of mission with him in Narok.

My good friend Andy Economides was planning a mission later that same year in Kakamega, Kenya. So he asked if I would visit the leaders in Kakamega after the Massai mission, to discuss plans for their mission.

So, early in 2001 I was met by David Kereto at the airport in Nairobi. He took me to the Hilton Hotel briefly while I had a coffee and he arranged transport to Narok. It's always good to clarify things in advance and this I failed to do. David turned up back at the Hilton with a matatu. Anyone who has travelled in one will now be laughing. For those not familiar with the concept, let me explain. 'Matatu', I'm told, means 'three times' – meaning the vehicle will hold three times what it was built to hold. Ours was an old Peugeot with three rows of seats. It should, at a push, hold seven people. We had ten people, two goats, three chickens, and two sacks of rice plus our luggage. The thing seemed to have no brakes and uncertain steering. The driver reached speeds that gave me to think he had a death wish. As we left Nairobi, we reached a mountain pass. We swerved round torturous bends at high speed, dodging oncoming traffic. At one point I felt we would plunge over the edge of the cliff into the valley below. I began to pray under my breath. David observed my discomfort.

"Relax man! This is Africa!" he reassured me.

Unconvinced, I continued to pray. Up ahead, the rains had washed away the tarmac. I felt sure the rough ground ahead would slow the driver down. No chance. He drove faster, if anything, as we bounced across the rough ground where the road had once been.

Round the next bend, I saw a huge lorry, stacked high with bananas, taking up the whole road. It headed straight towards us and was clearly not giving way to a matatu. The drivers seemed intent on playing 'chicken' – heading straight at each other. At the last moment, the matatu driver swerved off the road, across rough ground, and somehow swerved back onto the tarmac after the lorry had passed, without losing speed. I began to prepare for death, sure that we would never survive this journey. I saw women walking in the road with baskets on their heads. Surely he would slow down for pedestrians. Not a chance. The women scattered in all directions as our matatu roared past.

Finally, in the distance I saw a small man sitting by the roadside on a chair. As our matatu approached he raised his hand while staying seated. A simple and surely futile gesture. But the matatu stopped. The matatu stopped because this man was a policeman. What I learnt that day is that the devil may be driving us crazy and telling us we are going to die. But we need to take authority over the devil's madness in Jesus' name. Jesus has the authority to stop the devil driving you to an early death.

We reached Narok at sunset and checked into a small guest-house by the market. My room was opposite the loudspeaker in the tower of the mosque. Every morning at four o'clock I was woken by the adhan – the muslim call to prayer. And every morning it spurred me on to prayer – not to Allah but to Jesus. It made me realise that while there is revival in parts of East Africa right now, the enemy has sown 'tares' everywhere to grow up among the crops and strangle the harvest.

I was introduced to the committee organising the mission, which was a week of Bible teaching and healing ministry. The churches had built an inter-church meeting hall by the market place and the conference took place there every morning and afternoon.

I preached on John chapter seven, where Jesus says, "On the last day, that great day of the feast, Jesus stood and cried out, saying, 'If anyone thirsts, let him come to me and drink. He who believes in me, as the Scripture has said, out of his heart will flow rivers of living water.'" (John 7:37, 38)

I hadn't fully appreciated the difficulties in the local area. They had been through months of drought. The crops and grass had dried up. Cattle had literally died of thirst. People had been starving. As I closed the message, the rains poured upon the land. One Massai pastor stood up and declared "I am Lazarus! I was dead. The drought killed my faith in God. I was dead. But today Almighty God has sent you to bring life! To bring this word. To bring this living water. As you spoke, I drank in the spirit. I am Lazarus – four days dead but now I am alive again!"

A great prayer broke out among the people. All prayed at the same time: Kikuyu, Massai, English, Anglican, Methodist, Baptist, Pentecostal. What a sound. And the rain seemed to join us as it reached a crescendo – raining down on the corrugated iron roof.

Day after day we spent time in the word of God. Day after day, people were healed, set free and some gave their life to Jesus.

At the end of the week, I told David to hire a car for the seven-hour journey to Kakamega. He said it would be too expensive. I said I would pay. I was not risking my life in a matatu for seven hours!

The chairman of the conference committee asked if I wanted to see a real Massai house. He was a Kikuyu but his wife was a Massai and her mother lived the real Massai life in a remote place.

We drove for about an hour. The last mile or so was across open ground in the land of the Massai. The Massai are cattle herders. We saw an elderly Massai man approaching with cattle and the driver stopped in respect. This was the chief in this area. He questioned the driver and David about who we were. Then he smiled at me and gave his permission for us to continue.

We reached the home of the chairman's mother-in-law – a simple stick and mud structure – the 'manyatta' where she lived. They took me into the manyatta and explained what each room was. As there were no windows and it was totally dark inside, it was almost impossible to know when we went into and out of each room. There was a room next to the children's bedroom for newborn calves.

The old lady lit an oil lamp and pulled out a treasure chest from under her bed. She opened it with great reverence. Inside were all the ceremonial dresses and bangles worn by the Massai on special occasions. A large number of Massai children gathered round the house to look at these strange visitors but ran away, hiding their faces when I lifted my camera to my face. It was quite a day and such a privilege.

Next morning, we left early, in a car David arranged for us, for the seven-hour journey to Kakamega. Hour after hour, we travelled across the rolling hills of the Kenyan landscape. It was a beautiful day and I was glad to have a break from the ministry. Although it had been a great week it had been exhausting.

We checked into the Golf Hotel, Kakamega at Andy's suggestion. It was a great place. A simple hotel set in large grounds near a golf course. As the sun rested on the horizon and a gentle rain began to fall, I sat outside, under a veranda, and drank a freshly squeezed orange juice. Bishop Simon Oketch called and checked everything was set for the meeting of church leaders in the morning.

The next day, after David Kereto had left to travel back to Narok, we had a series of meetings with church leaders from all denominations in the city and various people took on tasks of co-ordinating various parts of the mission, which we set up for September that year. There was a great spirit of unity among the team and Bishop Simon and the Pentecostal bishop seemed to be the leading characters in the group. I left them with a lot of work and they left me with some questions to discuss with Andy on my return.

I made some enquiries and discovered that instead of an eight-hour car journey back to Nairobi, I could get a taxi for one hour to Kisumu and then fly to Nairobi in forty-five minutes, all for forty quid! It seemed too good an offer to refuse.

After landing back in Nairobi, I spent the night at the Hilton Hotel. This meant I slept, swam and had a hot bath and a decent meal before travelling back to the UK. It also meant I had time to think and reflect about the whole trip and the September mission details.

Back in the UK there wasn't much time to waste as I now had to prepare for a mission to Nigeria with Andy and his team. I travelled to Chichester for a day to be with Andy. Here I met the other team members, Jill Ford and Alison Payne, both students at All Nations Christian College. Jill is a great person to be with – an extrovert – we always laugh a lot when she's around. It was partly due to this that I didn't really get to know her quieter friend Alison. At the end of this preparation day, we had a team photo and then said farewell until the trip.

This second trip to Nigeria was as powerful as the first. It was great to work with Andy again and having two women on the team changed the dynamic of the mission. Jill and Alison had a great ministry to women and girls, in addition to ministering generally in the meetings.

In the middle of this mission, we were stopped in our tracks. One day we were on the way to speak at a meeting. As we approached a flyover all the traffic slowed and diverted off the main road. I wondered why. All I could see was a burning tyre in the middle of the road. The black smoke belched into the sky. Hardly a major roadblock. But as we drew nearer I saw something else in the flames. It was a tyre burning, but there was something else.

As we all fell silent and our driver apologised for the incident, I realised the burning tyre was wrapped around a person. We had witnessed a lynch mob.

When we looked at the papers the next morning, we read how there was a problem in the city of people snatching babies to sell on to rich people. The burning body we had seen was that of a woman pursued by a group who were frustrated by the police's inability to stop the child abductions.

The next day we were driving back from a church meeting when again we saw a large angry crowd blocking the road. We slowed to make our way through. As we reached the centre of the crowd, I saw a man sitting on the road, covered in blood. People were shouting at him. The tyre was already in place and someone had gone for petrol to start the fire. As we passed, he looked directly into my eyes. I knew these were his dying moments. I wanted to stop the car and get out – to intervene. But the crowd was very angry and I felt anyone who stood in their way would meet the same end. So we drove on.

In all, four people were burnt to death by lynch mobs that week, for child abduction. It's a picture I carry to this day, particularly that dying man's gaze. I saw the evil of the human heart – that one man can kill another in broad daylight. "The heart is desperately wicked. Who can heal it?" asked Jeremiah thousands of years ago. It confirmed to me that the world needs Jesus more than ever.

Gary and Joan Hulme had been supporters of our ministry for some time. They had asked to join me on a trip to Rwanda. So we found ourselves arriving in Rwanda having flown via Brussels with a Belgian airline. As we cleared immigration we joined the many other passengers waiting to collect luggage. After a few suitcases slid down the chute, the carousel was switched off. We were informed there were no other cases as most of the baggage had been left in Brussels. It would arrive in four days' time on the next flight. To say we felt disappointed would be an understatement. We only had the clothes we stood up in now for the next four days. All my toiletries were in my missing suitcase. We checked into a cheap guest-house where the only free item in the bathroom was a bar of carbolic soap.

However, the mission programme had been planned and I was speaking in Kigali the following day. We were due to travel up-country to Butare where I was due to speak at a week-long crusade in a football stadium. Now we had to delay our journey for several days while we waited for our luggage.

We had always run these missions on a shoestring budget so we had always stayed in low cost, and often rough, accommodation. The place we stayed in looked basic but clean. However, I woke every morning with groups of sores on my body as the bedbugs had been chomping my flesh in the night. The fact that I had no change of clothes made matters even worse. In the end we went to a big hotel in the city and checked in for the night. At least here we could take a proper shower or bath and eat better food. And avoid the bedbugs.

We travelled out of the city to visit the land for the school. Charles was in America for three years, so his brother Fred took us to see the land. It was really just a field of weeds and a few banana trees. The villagers came out to meet us in a small house

Charles' ministry was renting for a school. After speeches and some food, some of our sponsored children performed a traditional dance. The villagers seemed unsure of our motives. I stood up on a chair in the crowded room and spoke to the crowd. "Next time I come, you will see a school in that field!" I told them. It was a statement of faith with no evidence that it would be true. Actually, there were only the foundations the next time I came. But today, after many setbacks and trials, there is a school in that field where more than 700 children are being educated properly. It's the centre of a community. A beacon of hope in a dark place.

We got a call that our bags had arrived at the airport and went to pick them up. After wearing the same clothes for four days, I think I wore four different shirts that evening – just because I could.

We left next morning for the long drive to Butare where the local church was eager to welcome us. Pastor Paul Gasigi was the leader of this mission and a great encouragement. We laughed a lot together.

A new guest-house had been built in the town and our hosts suggested we should stay there. It was a simple guest-house but it was clean, sold good food and didn't have bedbugs.

The crusade kicked off with about one thousand people on the first night. Every day we saw people coming to give their lives to Jesus and people came for healing. One night, black clouds approached the stadium and some people ran for shelter. Pastor Paul urged them to stay and have faith. The ones that stayed witnessed a miracle. As I preached and called people to receive Jesus into their hearts, the rain approached but it seemed unable to enter the stadium. I looked around at the strange phenomenon. It was raining heavily on all four sides of the stadium but not in the stadium. It was one of the strangest things I have ever seen.

During the day I preached at meetings in Butare University where hundreds of students came to the meetings. One Friday we had a meeting at midnight in the university stadium. Again many people gave their life to Jesus Christ.

On Sunday, I preached in Paul Gasigi's church and many came forward for healing. Some who were healed of serious disease were so moved by God's love that they knelt down and wept tears of joy long after the service finished. We returned to Kigali for further preaching at the end of the week. We stayed again at the Hotel Des Mille Collins (made famous by the film 'Hotel Rwanda'). It was on this trip I decided that always staying in the cheapest place was a false economy. I wasn't getting any younger and, if I was to continue this overseas ministry, I needed to sleep well and eat properly. I came up to a new level of thinking. God isn't calling us to make the task of the great commission harder than it needs to be.

Chapter 26

The stretch limo and the giant cucumber

Dawn on a Tuesday morning. Somewhere over the coast of Newfoundland, I stirred from a fitful sleep in my economy class seat. I lifted the window blind to look out on the snow-covered landscape below the aircraft. It was my first sight of America. I looked with wonder across the frozen wasteland and thought of Columbus. For the only time in my life, I was flying alone. I had no one to share the experience with. Again I wondered at God's grace – bringing this boy from the Manchester backstreets all the way to America.

I had been invited by the Luis Palau Evangelistic Association to their Next Generation Alliance Conference in Fort Lauderdale, Florida. I would be joining about four hundred evangelists, mainly from the States, for a four-day conference and a chance to encounter Luis Palau's Beachfest event. Over 118,000 people would attend this two-day mission.

I was looking forward to seeing my good friend Charles Mugisha from Rwanda who was in the USA doing his Masters degree. He would be flying in from Portland, Oregon. I was arriving the day before the conference and would have to wait a day for the other evangelists to arrive.

I changed flights in Chicago and caught the connection to Fort Lauderdale. I don't know what

I was expecting but I arrived at midnight and found there were no cabs at the airport. As the other passengers met with friends and disappeared in various vehicles into the night, I began to wonder what to do.

I saw the Hertz car rental desk and asked the guy behind the desk if he knew where I could find a cab.

"There's no cabs at this time of night," he said. "Where you going?"

I showed him the hotel leaflet I had in my hand.

"Ah. You need to speak to Mickey," he said.

"Mickey?" I asked.

"Yeh. Mickey. He's from Morocco." He picked up his phone and pressed a number.

After a couple of minutes, in came Mickey.

"Hey. You wanna limo?" he asked.

"No, I don't want a limo, I want a cab." I said, sounding very English.

"You won't get a cab now," he said. "Where you goin'?"

I showed him the address.

"I can take you there for forty dollars," he offered.

Not knowing whether it was just round the corner or fifty miles away, I agreed. We walked out of the airport into the night. In the corner of the car park he opened the door to his stretch limo – an eighteen seater!

"I can't get in that!" I exclaimed. "I work in Africa!"

"Please yourself," he said.

Reluctantly, I climbed in the limo and Mickey from Morocco drove me down the freeway to the hotel. I began to realise I was having reverse culture shock. In the Third World we are shocked at the poverty. As I swept into the hotel forecourt in my stretch limo, I had been shocked at the abundance. I checked into my room and ordered a sandwich. I stood at the window, as I waited, and looked out across the city. I pondered on the limo and asked God what was happening.

I heard that still, small voice. "You need to think bigger."

Next morning, about four hundred evangelists came to Fort Lauderdale for the conference. By midmorning the conference had got underway. I met Charles Mugisha in the foyer. We shared a room for the duration of the conference. The conference was a great encouragement and inspiration as key leaders from the Billy Graham organisation and the Luis Palau Evangelistic Association led seminars in various parts of the hotel. In the evening, we all joined together in worship and Luis Palau shared his vision for 'Beachfest', which would take place that weekend. The weekend event would cost $2,000,000 and would reach into all communities at every level.

The following morning we were all taken to the beach for a 'walkthrough' of the mission programme.

The Skate Church had built a huge skateboard park on the beach. The main stage was being erected along with the huge sound system. Massive television screens were going up all along the beach. Pepsi Cola were one of the sponsors and in return had the monopoly for selling cola at the event. Projects for feeding and clothing the homeless were underway, as were many meetings with business leaders in the community.

Back at the hotel, seminars continued about every aspect of running an evangelistic ministry – personal integrity, fund-raising, building supporters, maximising your output and so on.

Also at the conference were Compassion International, one of the biggest Child Sponsorship organisations in the world. It was great to see how they promoted child sponsorship and I made many notes about changing the way we promoted our small scheme.

When the weekend came, we were bussed to the beach to join in Beachfest. In the Florida heat, more than 118,000 people came to the event, which was like a massive rock concert. As I walked through the crowd, I saw a giant cucumber and a huge tomato walking on the beach. The characters from the Christian series 'Vegi Tales' were running a children's ministry. The skate park and stadium were packed to capacity with young people. As I took my place near the main stage, I sat with Charles and a friend of his visiting from Rwanda. As he looked in astonishment at all the bikini-clad girls swarming the beach, he said, "My God! This is a mission to naked people!"

On the final morning, I had breakfast with some of the seminar leaders and Luis Palau's PA. It was a great time of encouragement and so inspiring to see someone of Luis' age make such a shift in approach – from crusades to festivals. It challenged me to keep open to new methods of sharing the unchanging gospel.

I left for the airport in a cab. Not a stretch limo. But although the cab was a lot smaller, I hadn't forgotten the lesson of the limo I arrived in. The word from God had been to think bigger. As I reflected on this inspiring trip, I came back from America with what I believed was a command from God to 'double the ministry'. I wasn't exactly sure what that meant in practice but I was determined to obey the call.

One of the most pressing things I faced right now was a lack of administrative help. One or two volunteers had helped out, but apart from my friend Ted, who managed our Gift Aid, we had little help. I know mathematically that double nothing is still nothing, but the spirit of God's command was to increase the ministry. Soon, I discovered my friend Claire Smith was looking for some part-time work. Within a couple of weeks of Claire working three mornings a week, she had a real grasp of how everything worked and was already suggesting improvements. To say Claire was efficient would be an understatement. This one change really began to set me free to focus on the bigger picture.

I had been taking time to keep in touch with Jill Ford and Alison Payne at All Nations, going over there for lunch every couple of months. Alison had wanted a contact in Uganda and I had connected her with our old friends at Gaba Community Church near Kampala. Alison asked if she could do missions under the RSVP banner, as it were. I agreed, with a few conditions. This led to a growing relationship between Alison and our work. During the three years Alison was doing her BA in Cross Cultural Missions, she led several teams into Uganda on RSVP's behalf.

One of the things I did in those days, when visiting the college, was to chat to various students about their future visions and plans. As Alison drew close to the end of her three years, I suggested various possibilities of fulfilling her vision.

At a meeting with Andy Economides, he expressed a frustration that we are always pointing people with potential to other organisations. He asked why we don't recruit these people for our organisations. It was as a result of that meeting we began to talk about Alison coming to work with us and Soteria Trust.

As a result of those conversations, and after a little confusion in the early stages about how it would work in practice, Alison did come and work for RSVP full-time. This was another way we doubled the ministry. We originally had one evangelist. Now we had two.

One question was how we would pay Alison. We didn't really have the finances. I told her to do what she could to raise support but leave room for God. As we stepped out in faith, I was sure God would act. At the point Alison started to be employed by RSVP we had less money in the ministry than ever before. A lesser man would have flinched. But I prayed like never before and God responded. The month Alison started with us, an old lady died and we received a letter from her solicitor saying that she had left £10,000 in her will for The RSVP Trust. That was such a boost to our faith. We have managed to pay Alison every month since that day without fail. God is faithful to those who are full of faith.

Chapter 27

Slums and studios

I had been concerned for some time about the growing numbers of street children on Rwanda's streets. I felt a call from God to build a home for some of them. We launched an appeal but the response was not enough. About that time, Alison went out to Rwanda on a mission for us. She met with Charles to talk about the street children. Between them they came up with a lower cost option. We could feed the street kids twice a week and have a worker dedicated for them at a cost of around £350 per month. I had no idea how we would raise that amount either but on the phone one morning to Alison, in Rwanda, I gave her the authority to go ahead and set it up.

From that day on, we have financed a street children rescue programme which now feeds about two hundred children twice a week. Some of them have gone on to be invited to live in orphanages run by other organisations. We continue to finance the feeding and care of the children. Today it costs us more because we found the children have medical needs and there is no NHS in Rwanda – their medical bills have to be paid or they stay sick or die. My dream is that one day, not one child in Rwanda will sleep on the streets feeling unloved and uncared for, open to abuse, addiction and starvation.

Everything we were doing in Rwanda was development, which tends to look at the long-term. But I kept coming across people who didn't have time for long-term solutions. Some people are starving today. Some people are dying of AIDS today. Children are becoming orphans today. For many people, the effects of long-term development projects will come too late.

It was thinking about these people that moved me to set up RSVP's Gifts of Hope Fund. Gifts of Hope is a simple project where we find a need and meet it now – immediately. If people are starving, we buy them some food. If they don't have a mattress and blankets to sleep on, we go and get them some. Need a couple of goats to breed so you can sell their offspring and make some money? We'll buy you a couple. Roof fallen off the house? We'll go and get some roofing sheets for you. It's not rocket science. It's not 'development'. But it is love in action. "Does the money get to the poor?" people ask. Yes it does. I take a few days in each mission. I go to the market. I buy sacks of rice, maize flour and other basics. I load the van with mattresses and blankets and I personally take the Gifts of Hope so our supporters know their gifts have reached the poor.

To date we have spent thousands of pounds making hundreds of people's lives a little bit easier. The stories we find in the slums always make me cry. I wish I could do more. But at least we are doing something.

Two people we met recently sum up Gifts of

Hope. I was taken my by friend, Specioza, to see a lady in the slums of Kigali. We knocked on her door. She lived in one room with two small children. The other room she let to another family to get a little money to live on.

"Her name is Angelica. It means an angel," Specioza told me. Angelica was a pretty young woman. As the story unfolded, I learnt that Angelica was raped by a neighbour when she was quite young. She became pregnant as a result. Then another man said he would take pity on her and moved in. She had another child with him. But now he had left and she was all alone with the children. They all slept on the concrete floor with one old ragged blanket between them. We gave her a week's supply of food, a mattress and some new blankets. It didn't solve all her problems but it brought hope to a hopeless situation.

Out in the village, on another Gifts of Hope delivery day, my friend Rebekah took me far into a village where there were no roads, not even a dirt track. We arrived at a small shack in the middle of nowhere. An old lady was sitting on the ground in front of the house, crying. As we climbed out of the van she cried, "I am so hungry!" She hadn't eaten for three days.

I told Rebekah to tell her that this was her day. We opened the back of the van and cut open the large sack of rice and another of maize flour. We gave her and her granddaughter plenty of food. I asked her if she slept on a mattress or on the floor. She smiled, hope shining in her old eyes. She grabbed my hand and took me into the house. She showed me three planks of wood resting on some old boxes. This was her bed. We brought two mattresses for her and her granddaughter and two sets of new blankets. When we went to leave, she was dancing in front of her house, singing a song of joy in Kinyarwanda. A short visit had turned tears to joy. Cost? Twenty-five pounds. I often cry when I get back to my room at the hotel after visiting people like Angelica and that old lady. Who am I that God should allow me the privilege of doing this work?

A few weeks later, in stark contrast to the slums of Kigali, I found myself sitting in the GOD TV studio in Sunderland with Rory and Wendy Alec, live on air. It was the GOD TV Battle for Britain weekend and I had been invited to talk about how God had changed my life. What a great privilege to share one's story. But what a greater privilege to share your story with people all over the UK.

Rory had told me that if I wanted to pray with people, to just go for it. I was a bit nervous as it was all live on air. As I got to the point where I was to 'go for it', I saw Rory nod towards a camera and signal to me. Just as he had explained to me before we went on air, I looked into the camera and led people in a prayer for healing from a broken heart and a prayer to receive Jesus into their life. It had been a strange week. I arrived back at the hotel in Sunderland after midnight. I flicked on the TV and watched a few minutes of 'Nuns on the Run' with Robbie Coltrane. I drifted into a fitful sleep, disturbed at various points in the night by dreams of men dressed as nuns, TV studios and many other thoughts all swirling together.

As I travelled back south the following morning, I wasn't sure if I'd obeyed the call to double the ministry but things were certainly growing and expanding.

Chapter 28

Why not here, Lord?

"Ladies and gentlemen, we are beginning our descent into London Heathrow. Please fasten your seat-belts and put your seats in the upright position."

It was 5.30am on a Wednesday morning in October. The Kenya Airways flight from Nairobi was beginning its descent into Heathrow, at the end of our eight-hour flight. It's never easy to sleep on a plane in economy class and I was tired after the long night flight home. It would be good to be home again and see Hazel and the girls. I began to think about the past two weeks. What miracles we had seen in Rwanda. More than two thousand people had accepted Christ in the meetings, in a single week. We had seen the blind receive their sight, the deaf hear, and the lame walk. I particularly remembered a large woman throwing her crutches into the crowd and marching in front of everyone to show she was healed. It had been like living in the Bible days – the stories in the Acts of the Apostles.

"Lord." I said under my breath. "Why don't we see such things here in the UK?"

Immediately I heard God speak to my spirit. "Well, you won't see such things here in the UK because you don't expect them to happen and you never give me time to work."

Ouch! I saw the truth of this statement straight away. How true it was. It seemed I was the blockage to seeing such miracles in the ministry in the UK. I repented there and then.

"Lord, from this day on, whenever I am asked to speak about healing, I promise to go with expectancy and, as far as it depends on me, to give you time to work."

As the days unfolded and I caught up with the office work, I noticed an appointment in the diary. I was to speak at an 'Evensong and healing service' in Norfolk. I thought about that promise I had made to God on the plane. I prepared a message for the service but more importantly I prepared myself. I went with expectancy and I went with a determination to give God time and space to work.

As I drove up to Norfolk, it was a bleak, dark night. The country lanes through all the villages were cloaked in rain and an icy wind made the temperature plummet. Through village after village, the cold and the rain threatened to drown out faith. Who would come out to a cold church on a night like this? I thought of the parish magazine they had sent me which, due to a slight typo, advertised tonight's meeting as 'Evensnog and healing with Don Egan'. I wasn't sure what 'Evensnog' was but I thought it might entice a few extra people.

After getting lost a couple of times in the East Anglian countryside, I finally found the church. I dashed from the car through the driving rain and opened the large wooden door to the church. A couple of men were handing out the hymn books and welcomed me. One of them took me to the vestry where I met with the vicar.

"I don't think we'll have too many tonight!" he said. "Not with this weather."

I tried to hold my faith firm. I had come expecting miracles but everything was coming against it. I asked if people would come forward if I offered prayer ministry.

"One or two," the vicar said doubtfully.

As the service commenced, I counted thirty shivering souls – God's frozen people. After a few traditional hymns and some 'Evensnog' liturgy, I stood to speak. "Lord, help me do this," I prayed in my heart.

I spoke briefly about the man let down through the roof by four friends, who was healed by Jesus. I talked about the many who hindered, the few who helped and the One who healed.

Then I offered to pray for any who had need of a miracle. Almost all the congregation came for prayer. There were two very notable miracles that night.

The first was a lady called Penny. She was suffering from Seasonal Affective Disorder – or SAD. It was a miracle she was there because SAD causes its victims to become seriously depressed from about October through to April. She told me that many days she couldn't even get out of bed. She had to sit in front of a light box to get well enough to do anything.

I laid hands on Penny and spoke a word of scripture over her – "Be transformed by the renewing of your mind."

Before I could pray, she suddenly said, "I'm healed!"

I didn't really believe it myself. I thought, maybe she's a bit odd. She went off telling people she was healed. She wasn't odd. She was healed. She wrote to me later that week and told me an amazing story of how she was completely set free. Her son also had the disorder, as did his seven-year-old son. But they were healed after hearing of Penny's healing. I saw her some months later at a meeting I was speaking at. She was still smiling and told me how the healing had totally transformed her life.

The second notable miracle that night, was a lady called Louise. She told me her daughter had become verbally abusive to her and her husband, wouldn't go to school without a fight and they were at their wits' end. Her daughter wasn't at the meeting but at home with her father, Louise's husband.

As I prayed I experienced a spirit of fear. It's hard to describe but it was as though God let me briefly experience what was wrong with Louise's daughter. I prayed to bind the spirit of fear and spoke peace on her house.

Louise contacted me the following week to say that when she got home that night, her husband told her that their daughter had a complete character change at about the time we had been praying. The next morning, as Louise was saying goodbye to her husband at the front door, they heard a voice behind them say, "Good morning Mummy and Daddy." It was their daughter dressed and ready for school. As far as I know, she's been fine ever since.

In other healing meetings since that night, I have seen a lady who was blind for forty years recover her sight. She sent me a little cross-stitch bookmark which I keep in my Bible. It reminds me that blind people don't do cross-stitch but that lady did because God healed her sight.

Everywhere I have been allowed to give God time and space to heal, and gone with expectancy, he has always showed up. One vicar allowed me to pray for the sick but asked me before the meeting, "What if nothing happens?"

I told him, "I can't tell you exactly what God will do or what will happen. But one thing I can absolutely guarantee is that something will happen because Jesus said, 'Nothing is impossible with God'." Nothing is the one thing that won't happen because that's impossible with God. Something has to happen. He was very happy, a week later when he wrote to me telling me of a blind lady who recovered her sight when she got home from the service.

The things we read of in the gospels should be the experience of all Christians because Jesus said,

> "I tell you the truth, anyone who has faith in me will do what I have been doing. He will do even greater things than these, because I am going to the Father." (John 14:12)

Chapter 29

Kestrels and kebabs

The early morning mist, illuminated by a hazy sun, drifted across Rutland Water. In the distance, the sinister black figure of a cormorant, with its wings held out, was just visible on the shore. Across the surface of the lake swooped a flock of black-headed gulls calling to one another. I pulled the zip of my jacket right to the top and took my cup of coffee in my hands, as I sat outside the lakeside cafe in the crisp morning air. I was waiting for my great friend Martin Garner to arrive. Rutland is just about half-way between Stowmarket and Sheffield, Martin's home town. Every six or seven weeks we meet here for a day. We talk. We have lunch. We walk along the shores of the lake and talk some more.

Martin is one of Britain's authorities on bird identification. If claims of rare bird sightings are made in the 'twitcher' community, he is often the man they bring in to confirm or deny the sighting. Presently, Martin arrived along with his spotting scope. As we walked and talked, he interspersed the conversation with a commentary of rare birds visiting from afar, or migrating to warmer climes.

Martin was at college with me back in my Church Army training days. But in recent years, after he returned from living in Northern Ireland, we had renewed and deepened our friendship. I believe

Martin is a great visionary for the gospel. He has planted several churches and led many people into a personal relationship with Jesus Christ. Our personalities are quite different and we seem to complement one another. I always find a day with Martin an inspiration. Some of our conversations at Rutland Water have triggered ideas for books, sermons and videos.

On this particular day, we both felt that God was calling us to work together more. As a result of this, Martin invited me to travel with him on a mission to Istanbul.

Martin had friends from a church in Istanbul which was struggling a little, in that overwhelmingly Muslim nation. A few months later I drove to Sheffield to stay overnight with Martin and his family before flying out from Manchester to Istanbul next day. At the time, Martin was employed on the staff of St Thomas Crookes in Sheffield. After arriving at Martin's house in the early evening, I went with him to his home group. What a mixed group it was. A couple of people seemed to be smoking dubious substances in the backyard. While indoors, a magistrate and a business man talked with others of very varied backgrounds. After sharing some food for a while, a group went into the front room to pray and worship. A young lady called Pippa would be joining Martin and me on the Istanbul mission and so the group prayed for the three of us. We also prayed for others who had needs before returning to Martin's house for the night.

Early next morning, we left for Manchester airport and caught the flight to Turkey. We arrived in Istanbul at night and waited around in the airport foyer for our contact, an American lady called Sue. Eventually she came and collected us from the airport and drove us into the centre of Istanbul. Martin and Sue caught up on news since Martin's last visit as Pippa and I sat in the back of the car, peering at the silhouettes of great ships on the Bosphorus sea. The roads were clogged with traffic as we got into the city and, as we crawled towards our destination, I could see thousands of people milling about and the many market stalls selling spices, busy with people. Eventually we crossed the city and reached the suburbs. We stopped outside a block of apartments and Sue walked us up to the home of Melek and her family.

Melek welcomed us in. We shared a meal and again Martin caught up with news as he introduced us. After the meal, Pippa and I stayed with Melek and her family, while Sue took Martin to stay with a group of students in another part of the city.

Outside Melek's apartment, opposite my bedroom window, was a large mosque. At about four o'clock in the morning I was awoken by a loud voice singing, "Allahu Akbar! Allahu Akbar!..." – the Muslim call to prayer. Melek had told me the night before about the feeling of claustrophobia many Christians have, because of the restrictive Muslim majority. Although technically a secular state, Turkey is 99 per cent Muslim, although very

European in its culture. Eventually the call to prayer ended and I prayed horizontally for a while before drifting back to sleep.

During the trip, we had various meetings with church members in small groups. They shared some of the difficulties they were facing in this anti-christian environment. As we talked, we asked people how they had come to know Jesus. Surprisingly, about two-thirds of them said they had started having dreams in which Jesus appeared to them and told them to follow him. Melek said, "What I noticed was that Mohammed did not appear in my dreams. Only Jesus. So I followed him!"

On the last night we were there, I was asked to share a word and felt a burden from God to share about overcoming difficulties. I shared my story about our son dying and how we found God in the midst of that tragedy. Some of the group sat open-mouthed as I spoke. I couldn't have known but one of the ladies had lost her husband, just a few weeks before, in a drowning accident. Her heart was broken and she was struggling to find God's peace. She told me in broken English that my message was so powerful and such a help to her at this time. I remembered the calling of God back in the Lake District – "...you shall go to all to whom I send you, and whatever I command you, you shall speak." (Jeremiah 1:7)

After the meeting, the Turkish Christians, and Sue, took us out for kebabs. It was nothing like having kebabs in the UK. It was a complete experience –

sitting in a restaurant in the middle of Istanbul with twenty Turks all ordering very interesting food and having a shared kebab which took up the whole of the table. What a great privilege!

Since that time, Martin has travelled with me to Rwanda several times and we have been together on mission in Northern Ireland. Our friendship has grown and deepened. I really view Martin as a 'soul mate'. He's a traveller on the same journey. I really appreciate him.

Chapter 30

The House of Mercy

Summertime in Suffolk. What a glorious season. I was sitting upstairs at home, in a room we have as an office. I was in the process of writing another book. The window was open and the occasional gentle breeze moved the warm air around. The birds were singing and I could see across all our neighbours' gardens. The trees and flowers were all flourishing and blooming. The birds were busy in the trees, as though sampling a royal buffet of berries.

I looked across the gardens and suddenly felt a great sadness. A little boy came to mind. I met him in the Philippines back in 1993. He was five years old. He stood out because all over his shaved head were small scars. I'd asked one of the ladies who ran the orphanage what these were. They were rat bites. This little boy had been abandoned by his parents and was found sleeping in the gutter. As he slept, the rats had been biting him. He'd been rescued a few days earlier and brought here to the orphanage for safety. The name of the orphanage was The House of Mercy. A tear fell from my eye.

"Why am I thinking about him, Lord?" I asked. I felt the Lord say, "I want you to build a House of Mercy in Rwanda." There were certainly many little boys, like that one in the Philippines, living on the streets in Rwanda. After some research I found there were more than six thousand children living on the streets in Rwanda, abandoned by the world. I had no idea how we would do this but, by now, I knew that God could do anything. I didn't announce anything just then but The House of Mercy vision grew from the seed of a thought into a vision.

A few months later I was visiting Rwanda with Martin Garner and Katie Johnson. We discovered that Charles was building a series of orphanages. He had built two and had sponsors for another two. He also had a plot of land to build a fifth one. I asked if RSVP could sponsor the building of a House of Mercy on this vacant plot. He happily agreed.

As soon as we announced the project to our supporters back in the UK, we received two gifts of three thousand pounds each, so work began. The total cost was around £25,000. We received a few small gifts but I couldn't really see where the money would come from to finish the project.

I sat down to write an appeal letter to our supporters. We needed about £15,000 to finish the building work. I'd just written, "Dear Friends" and was staring blankly at the flashing cursor on the screen, when the phone rang.

It was a man I'd met only recently at a conference. He'd read about our work and watched a DVD we'd produced on our work in Rwanda.

"How much do you need to finish your House of Mercy?" he asked.

"About £15,000," I replied.

"I can send you £13,000 if you want," he offered.

"Fantastic!" I said.

I didn't write the appeal letter. There was really no need. God has really sent people to support the work we do. I'm not allowed to reveal the identities of some of our donors because they want to remain anonymous. But I have to tell you, who God sends to give is often very surprising. To this day, I never cease to be amazed by how God supplies all our needs.

I have now been to the plot of land and stood inside the House of Mercy as the builders were putting in the windows and the door frames. I'm looking forward to my next visit to Rwanda when it will be open and caring for sixteen children. True, sixteen from six thousand street kids does not make a big difference. But it does make a big difference to the sixteen who are rescued. Our next challenge will be to find people to sponsor each child in the House of Mercy, to give them a future and a hope.

Sometimes people ask me, "Why doesn't God feed the starving and help the poor?" The people who ask that question seldom do anything for the poor themselves. My reply is that God does help the poor and feed the starving, but he uses people like me and you to do it. There is no reason, apart from man's greed and inhumanity, for any child to go to bed hungry today. If every well-fed person fed one starving person today, no one would be hungry. And I challenge you reader, what are you doing for the poor today? If you don't know how you can help the poor, send me £1 today, to the address on the back of this book, and I'll buy lunch for a street child. Send me £10 and I'll buy an elderly person a mattress and blankets so they don't have to sleep on the floor. Send me £18.50 a month and I'll send a child to school.

Staring out of the window that day in Suffolk, just taking a moment to be still, started a vision to build the House of Mercy. I don't know when you last stopped and stared out of the window or daydreamed for a moment, but I highly recommend it.

Chapter 31

Death at Christmas

Often in my life, I have found myself wondering, "What am I doing here?!" In the autumn of 2006, I found myself kerb-crawling, looking for prostitutes. It was all innocent and for a good cause. Alison who came to work for RSVP in 2003, had a way of pioneering new projects that linked us to people 'on the edge'. She spent one year at a local prison, lecturing to murderers and rapists who had opted onto a life-changing programme called the Compass Project.

After that was finished, she pioneered our work with prostitutes in Ipswich. The ministry had developed from the early days of Alison and her team walking the streets chatting to women 'on the game'. I remember the first night I went on the outreach. I went with Alison. Her husband Richard paired up with Nicola, one of our volunteers.

Alison and I met a young girl called Steph on one corner. I was shocked. She looked about seventeen or eighteen years old. She was dressed normally and looked like she was waiting for a friend. But she was waiting for 'customers'. She told the story of how she had been befriended by an older man whom she now lived with, who groomed her for prostitution.

Further down the road we met Tracy. She was

twenty-four and addicted to heroin. She had been introduced into prostitution at the age of twelve. Her mother had been a prostitute and her mother and father were both heroin addicts who died when Tracy was fourteen. She was swearing a lot and talking about suicide. She had a weeping sore on her leg as a result of injecting heroin. Further down the road we met two women standing together, which was unusual. They had not met the team before so we explained what we did. We offered them one of our goodie bags but one of the women, Tania, argued that they couldn't take all the goodies because they had nowhere to put stuff as their trousers had no pockets. They said they would have the sweets and the condoms but said they didn't want the booklet. Alison joked that, as I was the author of the book, the book was compulsory. They took the books but kept saying "Where are we going to put these?" As we walked off Tania shouted after us.

"Hey Don! I've found somewhere to put your book!" as she tucked it down the inside of her boot.

"Great!" we called back, assuming we would see them the following week.

Further down the road we met up with Gemma, who was talking to Richard and Nicola. Gemma knew the rest of the team so we talked for a little while. What struck me about Gemma was she looked so 'normal' and was very polite.

As we returned home, I realised this is what Jesus would be doing if he walked through Ipswich today – talking to real people with real problems and offering them real life.

The following week, Alison and I did the outreach from a new van which had been provided by one of our supporters. We saw a couple of the girls but the word on the street was that Gemma was missing and so was Tania. At the end of the outreach, we were about to go home when we saw a young lady standing alone in the darkness near the car showrooms. We hesitated. But we could think of no other reason for a young woman to be standing in this dark isolated place on her own. We stopped the van and introduced ourselves. The young woman was Annette Nicholls. She chatted for a while and had a hot chocolate with us. Soon we left her saying, "Take care" and drove off into the night.

I arrived home with my mind swirling. It had been a world I knew nothing about but I was sure we had to develop this part of our ministry.

"Police have found the body of a woman believed to be that of Gemma Adams who had been reported missing..." The breakfast news unfolded the horror that Gemma had been murdered. Days later more bodies were discovered. Over a ten-day period five women were murdered and their bodies discovered around the Ipswich area. Gemma Adams, 25, Tania Nicol, 19, Anneli Alderton, 24, Paula Clennell, 24, and Annette Nicholls, 29, seemed to have been murdered by a serial killer. Soon the area was swarming with news teams and media from the twenty-four hours news channels and all the national press.

I found it hard to comprehend, that these five young women – four of whom I had met – were now dead. Murdered by a serial killer. We had hoped to 'save' them in the spiritual sense. But now they were dead. I began to realise the great danger the women worked in.

Very soon the area was overflowing with media crews. The effect is hard to describe but it gave me some sympathy for celebrities who suffer constant intrusion from the press. The media soon beat a path to my door.

It felt like one of the most chaotic times of my life. We were in the process of remodelling the house – we had demolished the downstairs bathroom and replaced it with a conservatory. Plumbers were upstairs fitting the new bathroom. Walls were being demolished. Drilling, banging, shouting and hammering filled the house. I gave a short interview to the BBC Look East programme. The following day it all went mad. A man from SKY News knocked on the door at home. At the same time, BBC News 24 had got into the office and Beckie (my daughter and administrator) phoned to ask what to do. Soon the national papers were on the phone, all wanting to do an interview. A documentary maker from a well-known BBC programme offered me money to come on the outreach with me. I felt like saying, "No. You misunderstood. I am not a prostitute – you can't pay me money to make me do things. We are trying to rescue people from that! We can give an interview or not. You can give a donation or not. But you can't buy me!"

At this strange time, Hazel was away in Manchester, at a conference, and had rushed to her father's bedside as he was suddenly taken ill. He died in the early hours of the following morning. We now had our own grief on top of the local grief for the young women we were just getting to know.

Hazel's mother asked if I would conduct Gerry's funeral, so I prepared to join Hazel up in Manchester in a few days' time. Christmas was fast approaching. In the end, we had to switch the phone off and go into hiding due to the complete media frenzy.

The women were now running scared and afraid of being the next victim. Having lost their source of income, some were in urgent need of basic things. Alison and I visited some of the women at their homes taking basics like bread, milk and coal. We connected them with groups who would buy Christmas presents for the children and meet other urgent needs.

What irritated me during those days was all the news stories that talked about 'prostitutes'. These were women involved in prostitution but each one was somebody's daughter, somebody's mother, somebody's sister. 'Prostitute' was what they sometimes did, not who they were.

I travelled with my daughters up to Manchester and we checked into a hotel, ready for my father-in-law's funeral the next day. It was a difficult time. My feelings for the funeral were all mixed up with feelings about the murders. It was a difficult night's sleep.

Next morning, I arrived at the crematorium early. Although I had taken hundreds of funerals, I had not conducted one for a long time and the service had changed a bit since then. To my surprise, some of the crematorium staff remembered me from the days we were at Wythenshawe – twenty years previously.

Hazel's Dad was a very private man and I think few people expected the huge turnout for his funeral. The chapel was packed and many had to stand at the back. I think the person most surprised would have been Gerry himself. Christmas was on hold as we gathered to say goodbye. The British Legion standard bearer marched behind the coffin to pay respect to Gerry. It was a homely service made more intimate by the fact that his son-in-law was taking the service. Over refreshments after the service, Hazel and I caught up with various relatives of hers we had not seen for a long time.

We drove the 220 miles back to Stowmarket. It was Christmas Eve and we hadn't even thought about Christmas yet. As usual, Hazel went through the house creating a festive look and feel. When evening came, we kicked off our shoes and both nodded off in front of the TV.

After a few days, news came that police had arrested a man in connection with the Suffolk murders. Alison had kept a very detailed log of who she had met and when and where. This soon became invaluable to the police who used it to place the missing women at certain places and times before they disappeared. As the media interest subsided, the police interviews began as each murder was investigated separately. When the frenzy all died down and the media and police went away, we were still there on the streets – come rain or shine – offering unconditional friendship to broken women.

In the middle of all the murders and Gerry's sudden death, I'd gone with Beckie to my grandson's first school nativity play. It was a typical nativity with forgotten lines and amusing incidents. But, at the end of the play, the little boy who played Joseph presented 'Mary and child' to the audience and said, with great confidence, "This baby is God's gift to the world – and it's WONDERFUL!"

"Yes," I thought, wiping a discreet tear from my eye, "it is wonderful." Jesus came into our death and darkness – into the dark, sad, backstreets of this world. He is still coming here today. He is with us as we visit the women. He was with us at Gerry's funeral: "The light still shines in the darkness and the darkness has not overcome it."

Chapter 32

Heather and the snake

"It's time to go," I said, knocking on Heather's door at seven o'clock in the morning, at the Hotel des Mille Collines in Rwanda. We were on a mission to rescue 8,000 refugees from starvation. It was quite odd having Heather, my younger daughter, with me in Rwanda but it felt so 'right'. We'd talked about her coming with me on a trip to Africa for so long. Now it had happened. Beckie had joined me on a trip to Uganda when she was fourteen years old. Hazel had joined me to celebrate our twenty-fifth wedding anniversary. And now Heather, at last, had made it to Rwanda. I had successfully subjected all the family to my obsession with Africa.

Heather and I met our friend Charles Mugisha at the hotel entrance and began the journey to help the refugees. They had fled the war and genocide in 1959 and 1994. Now the government of Tanzania felt it was time they returned to their homeland and expelled them back across the border into Rwanda. They had settled in an area of bushland in the National Park, having few possessions other than the clothes they stood up in.

The countryside looked beautiful, bathed in the early morning sunlight as we drove to Kibungo district to meet up with the three tons of food we were supplying for the refugees. I'd promised

Charles I would bring at least £1,000 to help the people on this trip. Unfortunately, when I'd checked the bank account we didn't have enough money. I'd contacted one of our supporters who I thought could help. He'd generously given us £2,000 the day we left for Rwanda. I think my heart would have broken if we couldn't have helped these desperate people to at least be fed. The rain hadn't arrived and though they had planted the seeds provided by the government, nothing would grow until the rain came. They were starving.

Heather sat quietly in the back of the four-wheel drive. Charles and I chatted about our various poverty relief projects, as he drove. When we passed through the villages, groups of women and children gathered at rivers and pumps, collecting water for the day in bright yellow jerry cans. Some of them saw our white faces and stared at us. We were an ethnic minority here. The police waved us through various security checkpoints along the way. Eventually, we stopped at the school we helped build some years earlier and found the lorry almost loaded with the food. As the men loaded the last few sacks of food onto the lorry, Charles made a few calls to find out where the other team was. My great friend Martin Garner had joined me on this trip and brought ten members of his church in Sheffield with him. After about twenty minutes the minibus arrived from Kigali with the Sheffield team. The lorry was now loaded and ready to go. The convoy left the school grounds and drove a few hundred yards into town to meet the mayor. Charles, Martin and

I were welcomed into his office and he explained the situation of the refugees to us more fully. A lady who was the deputy mayor joined us and said she would be coming with us on the journey. She climbed into her official vehicle, and her entourage and some of Charles' workers followed in a car. Charles, Heather and I followed in the four-by-four. Then the minibus with the Sheffield team. Then the lorry with the food. Like a UN convoy we travelled further into a remote area of bush to look for the refugees. The tarmac soon ran out and the convoy created a growing brown cloud of dust as we drove mile after mile along the dirt track.

We passed through village after village of brown mud huts in this remote area. Many of the children had never seen a white man before. Children stood in the road, at the head of each village, saw us and began running ahead shouting to the other children, "Mzungu! Mzungu! Mzungu!" (White person). Crowds of children, waving and shouting, ran alongside the convoy. After about an hour, the dirt track also ran out and we were now driving across open bushland. There's a saying in Rwanda that a visit is blessed by God if he sends the rain with the one who is visiting. As we drew near to the refugees, amazingly the clouds opened and heavy rain – the long awaited rain – fell on the thirsty ground. The refugees greeted us with open arms. Not only had we brought three tons of food but, they said, "You also brought the rain!" Fortunately, the rain eased off during our visit. The local official showed us around the area. A school was under construction, as education was seen as one of the most urgent needs, even in these extreme circumstances.

We were taken to a jungle area where a space had been cleared so we could address the crowd. The mayor explained the procedure for the food distribution and gave other details of government action to help the refugees settle back in the homeland. About a thousand of the refugees had gathered. A generator and a PA system had been set up. Charles asked me to preach to them, which I wasn't expecting. "They are broken-hearted," he said. "We need to give them hope." As Charles introduced the team, a snake appeared in the crowd and everyone scattered. Three old men began beating the snake and killed it. Eventually, everyone came back and the meeting continued. I was introduced and greeted the crowd. It had been announced, "This is the man who is sending the food!" A great cheer went up. Yet again I tried to explain that although I was the one visiting them, it was people far away in the UK – RSVP partners and supporters – who were the ones supplying the food.

I spoke to the crowd on the words of Jesus. "If anyone is thirsty, let him come to me and drink." At the end of the message, about twenty-five people stood up to receive Jesus as their Saviour. I then prayed for the sick and there were some testimonies of healing right there. A small band struck up some Rwandan worship and soon the whole crowd was singing and dancing. Large African smiles lit up previously sad faces. We hadn't solved all their problems but we had brought some food for the next few days, a word of hope, prayer for the sick, music and dancing. Hope had come because someone cared enough to do something.

The day was far spent and a large red African sun sat on the horizon. We said our farewells and climbed back into the vehicles, driving through the now muddy tracks across the bush. This was the last day of a seven-day mission. It had been a busy week. As darkness fell during our journey back to the hotel and as Heather's eyes closed, after the longest day of her African adventure, I pondered on the many things that happened here because of my friendship with Charles.

I thought of the two hundred street children we feed every week. Of our visit to them a few days earlier. Of my tears when they gathered around us all and prayed for God to bless us. Of the boys who had come to me and said, "Sir, thank you for helping us when we had no one to look after us." I thought of the older boys in their blue overalls who were now learning carpentry instead of sniffing glue and shoplifting. I thought about the seven hundred children attending the school we had helped to build. I thought of the three builders I met who had been putting in the windows and door frames of the House of Mercy orphanage we had built. I thought about the thousands of people here who had read 'Yesu uramagira ute?' (What will you do with Jesus?) – a book I had written and which had been translated into Kinyarwanda, explaining how to receive Jesus. I thought of the three hundred children we have found sponsors for, who have real hope now because they can go to school. I thought of John, one of our first sponsored children, who had finished school with top marks and won a government scholarship. He told Heather, "Your Dad is not only your Dad. He is my Dad too. He's a Dad to many children here. He's a father to our nation." These and many other things stirred my heart. I knew we were far from finished.

God sent me here to help heal a nation. It's what I think about most days. I often cry when I come here. But not tears of sadness. I cry tears because I am moved by the love of the Living God who reaches down to bind up the broken-hearted, to feed the hungry and to breathe life into dead souls. He is a Father to the fatherless.

I cry because I am often moved that God has chosen to allow me the great privilege of being involved in this great work of revealing his Kingdom on the earth.

God has invited you to a party that is out of this world. He is waiting to hear if you intend to come. He is waiting for you to RSVP. And, in the meantime, he invites you to work with him to invite others and help the poor, who are precious to him. He invites you to remember the forgotten, love the unloved, and touch the untouchables. That's his invitation to you. It's time to RSVP.

Chapter 33

Who am I?

How can we sum up our life? For me, three words describe how I feel about myself: Fraud, Flawed and Faithful.

I've often felt a fraud because I find myself being thanked for things I haven't actually done. When street boys in Rwanda thank me for feeding and helping them, I am painfully aware that it is really our supporters back in the UK who pay for all this, and the workers in Rwanda who actually do the work. I am little more than a publicist or at best a motivator who persuades people to give to the work.

When a lady, who had been blind, thanked me that she could see, obviously I knew it was Jesus who needed to be thanked.

I also feel a fraud because, most of the time, I am wondering when the grown-ups will come and take charge of everything. I always feel I am making it up as I go along. Winston Churchill was told that one of his opponents was a very modest man. "Yes," he replied, "and he has much to be modest about." If I am honest, I often feel I have much to be modest about as well. More generally, I feel a fraud in that my public image always looks better than the real me. But I guess that's true for most of us.

Secondly, there are many ways I feel flawed. I often admire Hazel's faithfulness to me. I am not an easy person to live with. I would not want to live with me. Despite all that God has done in me and through me, I still have many moments of self-doubt, feelings of futility and a sneaking fear that, any day now, it's all going to go horribly wrong. Then someone who really knows what they are doing will have to come and put it all right.

Finally, I have tried to be faithful – faithful to God and faithful to life. Since that day, camping in the Lake District, when God first called me into his mission, I have tried to be faithful to his leading. At times of great decisions, it is always his still, small voice I seek to hear above all others. I want to be faithful to his word, to his teaching and to his life.

I am ready to step out of my comfort zone again and again to follow him. I have indeed forfeited my life that I may find it in him.

Often I ask the question 'Who am I?' It is not a question of identity – I am well aware of who I am. It's a question of who am *I*, to be involved in God's story, in his story? Like David, who began his working life as a shepherd boy and then became King of Israel. As he looked back from the throne to the sheep pen, he asked a question:

> "Who am I, O Sovereign Lord, and what is my family, that you have brought me this far?"
> (2 Samuel 7:18)

That's the question I am asking. And the only

answer I can find is that I am, indeed, no one. But God is no respecter of persons. If he did it for David, he'll do it for me. And if he did it for me, he'll do it for you. He is just looking for FATSOs – people who are **F**aithful, **A**vailable, **T**eachable, **S**pirit-filled and **O**bedient.

Hazel and I have just spent a week in the Lake District, hillwalking. Over the week we reached several summits. Some of the climbs were very steep. We stopped here and there on the way. We looked at the breathtaking views from various vantage points. We found unexpected beauty in secret places. We found lakes at the top of mountains. But there was always another summit to reach, always another mountain to climb. We had to press on. We encountered sunshine, wind, rain and gales. Our legs ached and sometimes we just had to stop and rest. We sat by small becks and babbling brooks, but eventually we had to press on towards home.

This year I reached my fiftieth birthday. It has been a time of reflection. I have come a long way from the back streets of Manchester. I have made missteps along the way. I have tried not to falter. As I think about my journey through life, I have just paused for a moment and looked at the view, as it were. Like King David, I glanced back to the sheep pen to see how far I have come. I looked back at the storms we survived and the steep climbs that stretched us. Many trials are now passed but this point in my life is not the summit.

I must turn now and look ahead to the next stage

and the next climb. I have come through the dark mists of Sinai and faced my sin before God's law. I have climbed up Calvary's beautiful slopes and found grace and mercy at the cross of my Saviour. But the climb continues, ever upward, towards the New Jerusalem. Till we come to the final summit and see Jesus face to face. "Here we have no abiding city, but we are looking for a city that is to come."

If you are a fellow traveller and coming up the slopes with me or after me, I hope you may find here a map to guide and encourage you. Don't give up. Press on, press on. I'm told the view at the top is well worth it.

Spiritual DETOX

Many people 'detox' their bodies but Don Egan says we need to detox our spirit – our heart. In this challenging book, Don tackles subjects such as anger, fear, pornography, forgiveness, hypnotism, the past, the future, and relationships.

"Toxic attitudes and actions have polluted our lives and relationships and we think if we just detox our bodies we will be healthier – Don Egan has hit the nail on the head in this refreshing and relevant book to help us detox our minds, hearts and our souls."
J.John

Search for God

Search for God tells four dramatic stories of how Jesus transformed desperate situations. A drug dealer, a model, a dying Hindu boy, and a rape victim who became an alcoholic, all encountered God in a powerful way. This is a great book to give to anyone who is... searching for God.

There are also Search for God 'give away' cards and a Search for God website. A great 'cringe free' way to share Jesus with friends and people you meet.

rhythm of LIFE

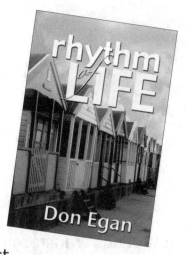

Man's first day on earth was a day of rest. We were designed to work from rest, not rest from work. This thought-provoking book from Don Egan explores the rhythm of life from birth to death, the rhythm of each day, week, month, year and season.

Don shows how we can tune into God's rhythm and find a new peace which will release greater energy and creativity in our lives.

"Fantastic! Everybody should read this book!"
Andy Economides

GRIEF
encounter

Is there life after grief? Can life go on? How can I find peace? Don and Hazel Egan's excellent book on finding hope in the midst of grief is used by many ministers when visiting bereaved families before a funeral. It tells the story of their son's death and the death of Don's parents, which all happened around the same time.

Drawing on these experiences and comforting words from the Bible, *Grief Encounter* includes prayers and advice on finding true peace after tragedy.

"A much needed piece of literature."
Victor Jack